WIT...
L. R. W9-AGV-166
...RARY

TARGET FLUENCY
Leading Edge
Foreign Language
Teaching Techniques

Michael Hager, Ph.D.

Metamorphous Press
Portland, OR

CARL A. RUDISILL LIBRARY
LENOIR-RHYNE COLLEGE

P
51
.H 27
1994
2 an 2002
A BN 2878

Published by
Metamorphous Press
P.O. Box 10616
Portland, OR 97210-0616

All rights reserved. No part of this book may be utilized in any form or by any means, electronic or mechanical, including photocopying, recording, or by any information storage and retrieval system, without permission in writing from the author.

Copyright © 1994 by Michael Hager
Editorial and Art Direction by Lori Stephens
Printed in the United States of America

Hager, Michael, 1954—
   Target fluency : leading edge foreign language teaching techniques /
   Michael Hager.
     p.   cm.
   Includes bibliographical references and index.
   ISBN 1-55552-068-5 (pbk.)
   1. Language and languages—Study and teaching. I. Title.
P51.G27   1994
418'.007—dc20   94-42199

TABLE OF CONTENTS

For my parents, Bill and Fay Hager

Foreword

Throughout my teaching career during the last 18 years, I have seen how important it is to be able to work well with people, to communicate with them and understand them. About seven years ago, I had an experience which made this even more clear to me. This is when I first got to know accelerated teaching techniques and Neurolinguistic Programming (NLP). Both provided me with keys to better understanding and communcating with people. I became aware of the fact that, as a language teacher, I was doing people work—therapy.

Thanks to the pioneering work of John Grinder and Richard Bandler, the co-founders of NLP, a whole new angle on psychology has been presented. This approach offered me new insight into teaching—and this book is the result. I have used the techniques presented here in various kinds of classes, from a "normal" class to a Suggestopedic one, from beginners to English for Special Purposes. I have used the techniques to teach English and German and have found that they work effectively for any kind of language or subject matter. I have also used these techniques to train teachers. The results I have been able to obtain have sometimes been astounding. Even when I presented this material at conferences throughout Europe, the responses from teachers in different countries were positive and the material was well received. This was gratifying, because I believe every teacher knows how hard it is to satisfy and please another teacher.

I hope this book will, at least, make you aware of the fact that learners are also only people, and that as teachers we need to respect and accept this. Of course, I also hope that the techniques will directly be of use to you in your teaching.

CHAPTER 1
Models of the World

In the early 1970s, Richard Bandler and John Grinder observed and modelled master teachers and therapists who where able to bring about rapid behavioral changes in their clients. Through these observations, they developed a model that teaches how to establish rapport, to gather information, and to detect and match a person's preferred method of communication. This model, Neurolinguistic Programming (NLP), also provides techniques that are designed to produce rapid and worthwhile interpersonal changes. NLP is a fascinating field that combines the study of nonverbal feedback and language patterns in order to better communicate and to produce rapid behavioral change (Cleveland).

NLP has been developed into a broad scope of various models, patterns, and strategies for behavioral change. However, here we will be concerned with the use of NLP in foreign/second language teaching, referring to the basics of NLP and some rather sophisticated techniques and their applications.

The human being is a creature that is infatuated with the construction and use of models. Since sensory organs are very different from one individual to another, we tend to perceive the world differently. These differences may be small or large. But because of this, it stands to reason that our models of the world will vary from individual to individual.

Bandler and Grinder have found that we filter the "information" used in our model-building process. There are three constraints that are applied to this process: neurological, social, and individual. In teaching a foreign/second language, our concern in this book will be with the last two constraints.

Through the sense organs and nerves, we initially receive information about the world. However, our individual differences and our translation of "raw" information into bioelectrical impulses separate us from the "real world." Because of our neurological filters and the differences of everyone's filters, it can be assumed that everyone's model of the world will vary. This leads to the belief that everyone does not react to the "real world" but to his/her own personal model of the world.

The second constraint is social. The primary example of this is language, which operates on our models of the world in two different and apparently opposite ways. Language both enhances and limits our perception of the world around us by encoding perceptual phenomena into words. Words are then manipulated by the mind in its effort to make sense out of experience. An example of this is the fact that Eskimos have some seventy different words for "snow." They are able to make distinctions about the quality and structure of snow that most other individuals in the world cannot.

The third constraint is individual and it results from personal experiences. These constraints are what form an individual's personal background. Individual constraints are based on neurological as well as social constraints. Continuing the process of construction and modification of a person's model of the world, the individual constraints form the fabric of the person's belief and value systems.

To better understand individual models of the world, the concept of internally generated stimuli is of importance. Every moment in time, the individual creates a "4-tuple" of experience. These are experiences of vision (V), sound (A), feelings (including tactile, proprioceptive and somatic experiences) (K), and olfactory and gustatory experience (OG). Each of us also possesses a great collection of stored experiences as memories, which can be shuffled, manipulated, and reorganized in very creative and different ways.

It is also possible to substitute at any time synthesized elements for other sensory-based experiences in a 4-tuple. This means that a person can experience a combination of internally-generated images, pictures, sounds, feelings, smells, or tastes in connection with external stimuli. For example, hearing your favorite song of fifty years ago can bring back beautiful internal pictures, feelings, sounds, smells, or tastes. These are based on individual personal history and will vary from person to person.

This concept is of great importance for every teacher, not only the language teacher. We are working with individuals, no matter how old or young, and must keep this individuality in mind. As well, these individuals are coming from different social backgrounds which influence their response and reaction to various kinds of stimuli. In general, each and every student is unique in his/her own way, and we as teachers must be able and willing to accept this fact.

STATES

At any given point in time, each individual experiences various neurological processes going on within her/him. These various processes accumulate to produce at one given time a **state**. These states we experience may provide us with the feeling of power or limit us in our abilities to do something. Whatever effect states produce in us, it is clear that they are usually unconscious reactions to that which we see, hear, feel, smell, or taste. Therefore, we need to learn how to be able to pick the states we need or desire. Lofland maintains that "a fascinating characteristic of states is that not only the brain experiences that state, but also the whole body experiences it" (p. 6).

Every one of us changes states unconsciously in reaction to people or situations around us. Two important elements in consciously being able to change states are:

1. **Physiology.** How do we perceive our physical reactions? How do we feel and carry our bodies? What are our emotions like at the moment? Being aware of such things in a given situation provides us with the chance to be able to change these characteristics to our advantage or to be able to use those positive characteristics in a less positive situation to change it.

2. **Internal representations.** In what way do we represent our model of the world internally/mentally? Lofland states that "our senses also create a model. When light hits the retina of the eye,

an electrochemical impulse travels to the brain. The brain doesn't directly perceive the light, but rather the electrochemical signal" (p. 8).

We can have various states depending on the input. It goes without saying that these states can be either positive or negative. In a positive state, you are at your best in a given situation and you know it. Whatever you do in this situation, you just seem to do everything right. By noting all the characteristics of this state you can become aware of the characteristics of your **resource state.** However, in another situation, no matter what you do, it just seems to go wrong. You just do not seem to be able to shake it. This state just hangs on. This is your **stuck state.**

Think of your favorite hobby. It is easy for you, you enjoy doing it, and you even have fun learning new things for it. You are "into" it; you are in the right "state." Now think of something you despise doing—for example, learning a foreign language. In this kind of state, you are not able to do much of anything, let alone learn easily. However, you can learn how to change your state. This can be done by changing your physiology, your internal representations, or both.

REPRESENTATIONAL SYSTEMS (VAK)

It has been found that each individual has five primary ways of experiencing the world: seeing, hearing, feeling, smelling, and tasting. (of course, these depend on the person's health and physical well-being). For our purposes here, I will combine feel, smell, and taste as kinesthetic.

Each of these sensory channels has a physical location in the brain where the experience is sent, processed, and stored. Our assimilation of this input can transform the information into something different from the original. What we later recall is a representation or model of that what our sensory organs transmitted to us. Each model can be referred to as a **representational system** (Lewis and Pucelik, p. 31-32).

Through various studies, Bandler and Grinder were able to establish two factors about a person's behavior that are essential knowledge for the language teacher: eye accessing cues and predicate patterns.

Eye Accessing Cues

Using video recordings, Bandler and Grinder observed their clients' eye movements and found that there was a correlation between how their eyes moved, how they were processing, and what they were thinking at the moment.

Jacobson states that these eye movements are as follows:

ACCESSING CUES	REPRESENTATIONAL SYSTEM
eyes up and to the left	eidetic imagery
eyes up and to the right	constructed imagery
eyes level and to the left	recalled auditory
eyes level and to the right	constructed auditory
eyes down and to the right	body sensations

For most beginners in NLP, it's easy to remember that eye movement up means visual, eye movement level is auditory, and eye movement down to learner's right (your left) is body sensation or kinesthetic. Body sensation is perhaps too generally put because it can also refer to emotions and feelings. Looking down to the learner's left indicates he is talking to himself (internal dialogue). (See face in Fig. 1, p. 6.) According to Andreas and Andreas (1989), these patterns apply to about 95% of all normal right-handed people.

Physical Characteristics

It has been found that posture can provide clues to whether your student is processing in a Visual, Auditory, or Kinesthetic mode.

Lewis and Pucelik expand on how, for example, a visual person in a stressful situation would pay most attention to the visual aspects of an interaction. These can include facial expressions as well as other gestures and movements around the visual person, not to mention his own internally generated visual imagery. It is also possible that the visual person will place himself at more of a physical distance from his partner(s) so he can observe most, if not all, of those who are taking part

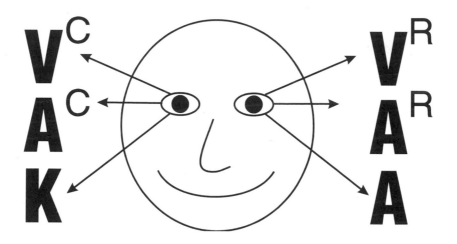

Figure 1: Eye Movement Patterns

in the communication. Sometimes this person will appear to be "looking down on" others so she can get in the right position to *see* what is transpiring.

Lewis and Pucelik point out that positioning for "auditories" is less consistent, but auditory people will position themselves within good hearing range. Auditories tend to keep their eyes lowered and away from the speaker—this helps them to keep from being distracted while listening. It is also possible that an auditory person will lip or repeat what he has just heard in order to better store the information.

Lewis and Pucelik maintain that "kinesthetic" persons rely a great deal on their feelings to make sense out of what is taking place around them. They also tend to place themselves, when possible, near enough to those with whom they are communicating so as to be able to touch them (pp. 57-58).

This does not mean that each individual exclusively uses one mode or the other. The activity in which the individual is involved is an element in determining which mode will be implemented. For example, a telephone call, for obvious reasons, will tend to be primarily auditory.

In her book *Influencing With Integrity,* Genie Laborde points out that facial color can also indicate which mode we are in at the moment: pale—visual; slightly red—auditory; and red—kinesthetic.

Cleveland believes that even gestures can "indicate which particular sensory system is being activated. In fact, they (students) will often touch the part of the body or organ which illustrates the sensory system. The student who rubs his eyes when you are talking to him may not be able to 'see your point of view'" (p. 56).

Predicates

Through various studies, it also has been ascertained that the predicates we use can be clues in knowing how we process information. The categories Visual, Auditory and Kinesthetic also apply here. For example, words like *see, observe, look, sight, picture,* or *view* are visual; words like *listen, hear, sound, sing, whisper* or *speak* are auditory; and words like *feel, touch, love, caress* or *walk* are kinesthetic. It has also been found that eye movements normally correspond to these words. That is, when a speaker says, "I see a bird," his eyes move up to the visual area. When he says, "I can't hear you," his eyes stay level (his auditory area), and when he says "This feels so good," he moves his eyes down to his right (his kinesthetic area). (See Fig. 1.)

Cameron-Bandler states that when listening to a person's predicates and watching his accessing cues, you will sometimes notice that these do not coincide. For example, the person accesses visually but talks about her feelings, or accesses kinesthetically and talks about how things look to her. Any other combination is possible. This tells you that the person uses a different system when she first starts to access internally stored information (this is referred to as the person's *lead system*) than her primary representational system. The person is accessing information through one system but bringing the information into consciousness through another.

Working with the representational systems allows the teacher the chance to know what kind of learner each of his learners is, or at least to be aware that the class has all of these different kinds of learners. The extent of difference is difficult to say, but it has been stated that most learners with learning deficiencies tend to be kinesthetic because present-day methods of teaching totally or almost totally neglect them (Michael Grinder).

The use of the VAK system can provide the teacher with ideas on how to teach in the most effective manner. If the teacher knows which system is preferred by which student, he can adjust his language accordingly, using visual words with visual students, auditory words with auditory students, and kinesthetic words with kinesthetic students. Being aware of this you can be cautious to not use only *your* own preferred system. Your preferred system is not the preferred one of everyone else!

Dawna Markova goes into great detail describing which kinds of learners there are and how it is possible to distinguish each kind of learner and which VAK system she prefers.

Michael Grinder also states that when working individually with a student, it is of essence to know the student's preferred system so that the teacher can position himself in relation to the student accordingly. For example, for visual students, the teacher should stand in front of the student so that the student can get a clear picture of what is being communicated. For auditory students, the teacher should stand next to the student so that she can hear clearly what the teacher is telling him. And for kinesthetic students, the teacher should stand near the student and help the student feel what is being communicated. (For a demonstration, the teacher should physically assist the student in going through the demonstration.)

For language teachers, it is possible to do various activities in the language classroom to implement the VAK model. When you are teaching vocabulary, write the words on flashcards and then cut up the words so that each letter of the word is on a separate piece of the paper. Then you have the student or a small group of students put the words together with the correct spelling. I use different colors of paper, one color for one word. It is also possible to have different words for different groups, and once every group has successfully spelled their words, a list of all the words is put up for the whole class. Then one member of one group claps out the number of letters or number of syllables in the word and the others must find out which word it is. You can also use the same list of words and have one student stand in front of the list, facing it. With one student directly behind the other student, the second student writes one word from the list on the other's back. The other student must then decide which word it is. (This can also be done for the ABC's, colors, etc.)

It is also possible to give a group of students a sentence and each student must pantomime one word or short group of words, i.e. a prepositional phrase from the sentence. (These words are put on different colored cards; i.e., one color for one sentence, but separate cards in the color group for each word or group of words.) Of course, this pantomime can express the student's feeling or relationship to the word as well as the meaning of it. Once all words have been pantomimed, the teacher has each student go inside himself and visualize himself forming the word or pantomiming it, listening to any sounds in his mind's ear, and feeling how it feels while forming the words or doing the pantomime. Once all words have been pantomimed, the students with the same colored cards come together and build a sentence from all the words. They then line up and hold their words in front of them, and each student says his word or group of words for the sentence. Thus the complete sentence in presented auditorally.

This process of "going inside oneself" and reliving what one has previously done or what one may be doing at the moment or in the future is referred to in NLP as a trance state (another word for this is daydreaming).

Hutchison points out that techniques such as trance states increase a person's brain fluctuations and consequently his ability to learn better and more quickly (pp. 88-89).

Learning a song can be used for all VAK systems. Once you have learned a song, have groups of students act it out or mime it and then draw a picture of their experience of acting out the text of the song.

For more advanced students, it is possible to make them aware of the different representational systems they use. The following exercise provides them with the chance to ascertain their preferred system and which system is weak.

To start, you must have groups of four. One person stands in the middle of the group and tells the others about a place she enjoys or finds interesting (the countryside, Finland, forest, etc.). Each of the other three students picks one of the representational systems (Visual, Auditory or Kinesthetic— olfactory and gustatory are included in Kinesthetic) and uses that mode to tell the person in the middle about his or her selected place. For example, if the person in the middle is speaking about the countryside, the "kinesthetic" person might say things like, "You are walking in the countryside and feel the grass under your feet. The sun is shining warmly on your body. It feels so good in the countryside." The "visual" person might say, "You see the beautiful colors of the countryside—red, green, blue, yellow. And you look at the beautiful blue sky and see little white fluffy clouds. Between the clouds, you see birds flying." Once each person has done his system for the person in the middle, the person describes how it was for her and then the positions are changed. A different person moves into the middle, and the others decide on a representational system (one they haven't already had). Once everyone has had the chance to be in the middle, have your students draw a picture about their experience in the middle and explain it, or write a poem or story about their experience.

The following exercise gives your students the chance to work with eye accessing cues. First explain the smiley face to them (see page 6). Then introduce sentences that will allow them to produce the eye movements.

Visual construct (Vc).
See a green cow.
See yourself without hair.

Visual reconstruct (Vr).
What's the color of your mother's eyes?
What does your bedroom look like?

Auditory construct (Ac).
Listen to your voice, ten years from now.
Listen to a rocket going into space.

Auditory reconstruct (Ar).
What does your mother's voice sound like?
Sing "Happy Birthday" in your head.

Kinesthetic (K).
What does it feel like to take a warm bath?
How does it feel to walk on a warm beach?

To personalize this exercise, have the students break up into groups of four or five and think of their own questions or commands. If you are working with beginners/intermediates, have them think of commands; if more advanced, questions, or a combination. Once your students have written down their questions (each one in the group must have a copy of the questions), have two people work together, but no two people from the same group together. One person in the group asks the other his questions or commands but does not expect a verbal answer. The person asking questions watches the eye movements of his partner and notes them down. After they are done, have them talk about the results.

For many kinesthetic students, it is very difficult to sit for long, so let them get up, walk around, or eat or drink during the lesson. However, be sure that they do not wander in front of the visual students or come in physical contact with them (this will shake up the visual students' pictures). As well, they should not be loud about walking, eating, or drinking as this will disturb the auditory students.

ANCHORING

An anchor is anything that produces a consistent response from a person. This can happen through any of our sensory channels. According to Lankton, "Natural language is a complex system of anchoring. To make sense of a given word, you must access past experience(s) and form a gestalt of sensory information" (p. 55).

Lankton also points out that anchors vary from culture to culture. In the United States, for example, the averted eye contact of a passing woman means something entirely different than the same behavior in the Middle East. Anchors are stimuli which are coupled with a rather predictable set of response (p. 56).

Michael Grinder claims that NLP has not invented anything new but has found patterns of effective communication and of identifying ways to transfer these patterns from people who have them to people who want them. Anchors stimulate an appropriate response in the affected person and can be simple, everyday things from the siren of a fire engine to a red light at an intersection.

Linda Lloyd points out, "Your words of praise, your smile and touch are all anchors, as is that certain tone of voice you use to let your students know you mean it and they had better behave. Any stimulus that gives a consistent response is an anchor" (p. 131).

In NLP terms, an anchor can be in any one of these three modes: Visual, Auditory or Kinesthetic (VAK). A kinesthetic anchor has perhaps the most powerful effect because you can be sure that the student has perceived it—with a visual or an auditory anchor, you cannot always be so sure. However, in today's society, kinesthetic anchors are usually not allowed, and it may be difficult or impossible to kinesthetically anchor something in a group of thirty students. Visual or auditory anchors are more appropriate.

Almost everything that teachers do in the classroom can function as an anchor—either positive or negative. Sometimes we are not aware of the fact we are doing something to trigger an unwanted anchor—a student may have had a particular stimulus negatively anchored by another teacher. Therefore, we must be flexible enough to accept the fact that we are not able to be in total control of these situations all the time (van Nagel, et al.). We are only human! Let's now take a look at how teachers can work with anchors in the classroom to produce positive results.

Perhaps one of the most important anchors is where you stand in the classroom when you are doing a particular activity. For example, if you are angry at the whole class, you should stand in one particular place to express this and not reprimand your class from various places in the classroom (personal communication, Michael Grinder).

Jensen states that "this strategy anchors the spot to what you are saying, you have created an association, a stimulus response with the location and type of message. In the future, because of repetition, you can simply walk to that part of the room and get the outcome you want" (p. 111).

The location of posters, charts, and other paraphernalia in the classroom also functions as an anchor. Hang your posters or charts in the same location in the room all the time. Grammatical charts with new information can be hung in the front of the room towards the upper left corner. Each time you have a new one, put it in this place. Your students will quickly realize that this is the location for new grammar points.

It is also possible to anchor a grammatical point with colors. In German, there are three different genders (masculine, feminine and neuter). For most non-native speakers, learning the genders is a difficult task, so have your students use colors for the different genders. Masculine can be blue, feminine pink, and neuter green. Have your students mark all masculine nouns with blue, feminine with pink, and neuter with green in the texts being used. Whenever a student makes a mistake with gender, merely indicate the color and the student knows her error. This form of anchoring (working with colors) also appeals to the right hemisphere of the brain.

Cleveland believes that anchoring can also be used for bulletin boards. Here it is important to remember the eye movement chart from Figure 1. By placing material to be remembered in the upper left-hand corner, the student has it already positioned for him in his visual reconstruct area. For instructions or materials that are imaginary or have to be constructed, the upper right corner is appropriate, as it coincides with the student's visual construct area. Kinesthetically-oriented material such as projects should be located in the lower right-hand corner, placing them in the student's kinesthetic area. Locate all other material or instructions in the middle "level" area to place them within the learner's auditory area. This pattern can also be used for the development of worksheets (p. 60).

Hager (1989) found that using anchors and representational systems can be very helpful in learning verb forms. To learn the different tenses of irregular verbs, create posters with lists of the various verb forms. These posters should be very colorful and offer the lists of verbs as well as pictures that correspond to some of the different words in the list. This functions as a visual anchor, and to make the effect even more powerful, have the students visualize the poster with their eyes closed. They can then open their eyes and compare their internal picture with the external one and correct any variations. To anchor this kinesthetically, they can dance to pop music (melody only) and chant the different forms of the verb (auditory anchor).

In German, it can be very difficult for students to learn the distinction between the two-way prepositions. For example, in one case the preposition "in" takes the accusative case when motion or action of some kind is involved (*Ich gehe ins Kino*—I go into the cinema). In other cases, where there is no change of position or motion, this preposition takes the dative case (*Ich bin im Kino*—I'm in the cinema). Learning this distinction is hard for non-native speakers of German when the distinction does not exist in their native language.

It is possible to make this distinction clear and simple by using anchoring and representational systems. Designate two different places in the classroom for this exercise. One will be an anchor for the dative case and the other for the accusative case. (Before doing this exercise, you should have already covered the accusative and dative cases.) At the location for the accusative, set the scene by telling your students they are standing in front of a movie theater. Have them go into a trance state and check all the pictures, sounds, and feelings in front of the theater. Then have them slowly open the door to the theater and walk in. As they are doing this, say, "Wir gehen ins Kino" (We are going into the cinema), emphasizing the "s" in "ins." While going into the cinema, your students should be doing a VAK check.

Once you have completed this, move to the dative location where the chairs are arranged like in a cinema. You all sit down and enjoy a film, and check your pictures, sounds and feelings in the imaginary cinema. While your students are doing a VAK check, say "Wir sind im Kino" (We are in the cinema), this time emphasizing the "m" in "im."

Depending on your group, you can do several more of these exercises for other two way prepositions. Once you have completed this, ask your students what the difference is between the pair "ins" and "im" and let them figure it out.

Later you can use the different locations as an anchor for accusative and dative. I usually have these locations already anchored for dative or accusative when we learn the two different cases to begin with. Once I start this exercise, my students already know that we are doing something with the dative and accusative cases.

Thus far we have seen how you can use anchoring in a positive way. It can be used negatively as well. When you shake your finger at a student, this is a negative visual anchor. When you click your tongue in the right rhythm and pattern, every student knows this is a negative auditory anchor for something he shouldn't have done. Further, any physical gesture you use where you physically touch your student can function as a kinesthetic anchor.

Magic Buttons

To counteract negative situations, you can anchor a positive situation that can always be activated when confronted with a negative situation. Van Nagel et al. refer to this as the "magic button." Their definition of a magic button is "pre-established anchors for positive states. For example, a person may be guided to recreate a pleasant, relaxed experience with the same feelings of calmness and confidence originally felt. These feelings may then be anchored by pressing a special spot on the body. This kinesthetic anchor or 'anchor button' then may be used by the person to recreate the positive internal feelings whenever desired or needed" (p. 48).

To create a "magic button," first decide where you can easily press a part of your body, a part that is easily accessible in any kind of stressful situation. Your earlobe is perhaps a good point. Now you want to think of a very pleasant and calm situation in your past. See all the pictures from this situation as clearly, brightly, and colorfully as possible. Notice any sounds in the situation (voices, music, birds singing, etc.). Finally, check your feelings in this situation. By doing these three steps, you are checking your visual, auditory, and kinesthetic systems to get a complete picture, sound, and feeling on the situation. Once you are totally into this situation, gently press your selected point for a minute or so. In order to check the magic button's effectiveness, think of a stressful situation, and once you are totally into this stressful situation, press your magic button and enjoy the positive effect. If there is little or no effect, you need to strengthen your magic button—the stressful situation is more powerful than the positive situation. You need to stack one or more positive situations on one magic button to be more powerful than the stressful situation. Do this by repeating the preceding steps for the magic button but for a different positive situation. Anchor this situation at the same position on your body as the others. Each time, test your magic button to see if it is powerful enough.

Doing this with students who are about to take a test can have a very calming and beneficial effect on them. Have them anchor a calm and pleasant situation and test the strength of their magic button. If needed, have them repeat the various steps until their magic button is powerful enough to overcome the stress of test taking.

Richardson gives a good word of warning in the use of anchoring: "Because anchoring is such a powerful process, and therefore of all the techniques we have presented so far offers the greatest opportunity for misuse—manipulation in the negative sense of the word—we advise you to be particularly careful when and how you use it. Remember, misused tools can boomerang. Your self-respect is one of your greatest assets; if you lose it, you've lost just about everything" (p. 122).

LEARNING STRATEGIES

It's understandable that good learners must have very effective strategies. Through the use of NLP, it is possible to observe effective learners and pass their strategies on to those whose strategies are not as well developed.

Mapping or recording a student's learning pattern by observing and matching predicates and eye movement is essential. In addition, the teacher must also ask the student (the effective strategy user) direct questions about his behavior. Van Nagel et al. give a good example of this:

Teacher first establishes rapport with student—

Teacher:	Billy, you can tell me about a time when you were able to do some part of arithmetic well?
Billy:	Hmmm, I learned my addition facts to 100 well. (Eyes went up to observer's right.)
Teacher:	How did you learn them so well?
Billy:	I'm not sure, I just studied them. (Eyes move upward and to the observer's right.)
Teacher:	How did you study them?
Billy:	My father held them up on flash cards, and I looked (Ve) at them, then said (Ae) them. He then took them away, and I'd picture (Vi) them as I wrote (Ke) them down. I really don't know how I learned them" (p. 137).

Even though Billy isn't aware of how he learned his basic addition facts, the process is easily observed. His learning pattern is Ve -Ae - Vi - Ke (e = external, i = internal).

In order to assist those learners who are having difficulties, teachers should be able to teach learning strategies (i.e., a sequence of senses used externally and internally). Billy may picture the facts and talk to himself as well as physically move through some action to complete the task at hand. This is a learning strategy that can be taught to others.

June Jackson has found that children can be taught an effective strategy for processing instructions. In her work, she has found that learning-disabled youngsters often focus their attention on stressful feelings and internal dialogue when confronted with the beginning of a task. In order to successfully follow instructions, it is essential to visualize what has to be done. This is likely to be left out of the strategy completely because the person is busy internally feeling his feelings, or talking to himself, or both. The result is poor comprehension or storage of instructions.

However, when a learner creates a visual image of completing a task, it is simple to "see" if more information is required, resulting in immediate feedback before mistakes are made. In a sense, this functions as a trial-run.

Verbal Instructions

First, give instructions to the learner. Second, have her look up and to her right and see herself doing the task. As soon as she has completed that, she can do the task at hand. If she has any questions about her pictures, clarify them and have her repeat the process (Jackson).

Written Instructions

Begin by having the learner read single instructions. Second, looking up to the right, the learner visualizes himself doing the written task. If he has questions about the process, answer them and repeat the process.

As the learner gains confidence, additional instructions are given. Soon the learner is able to picture himself doing several things sequentially in a successful manner (Jackson).

Visual/Auditory Integration Strategy

In order to effectively recognize a letter, phonetic pattern or word, visual/auditory integration must take place. Once the neural pathway becomes established and automatic, it can slowly be deleted.

STEP 1: The teacher says a word and shows it on a flashcard—with her hand, she indicates the different syllables. The teacher then removes the card and indicates again the syllables as the learner visualizes them and reads them in the air (at a moderate speed but not too slowly).

STEP 2: The teacher says the word 2-3 times at a moderate pitch and speed while showing the card. The learner just listens.

STEP 3: The teacher says the word (still at moderate pitch and speed) while showing the card. The student repeats word as he sees the card.

STEP 4: The analytical process is transferred to recognition. The word is placed directly in front of the student, and the student is told to "see it and say it" (Jackson).

Spelling Strategy

Learners often have problems with spelling, either in the mother tongue or in the foreign/second language. In NLP, there is a spelling strategy that works wonders for all languages. This spelling strategy is taken from a seminar folder developed by Charles Faulkner.

STEP 1: Ask the student to perform some task requiring visualization (for example, "Describe a movie you saw recently"). While the student is doing this, watch his eyes. The place where his eyes normally locate is his visual recall.

STEP 2: Ask the student to now see something in his mind's eye that isn't real ("Can you imagine a purple cow on rollerskates?"). The location of the student's eyes indicates his visual construct area. Go through Step 1 and 2 several times with different questions to be sure of the two visual locations.

STEP 3: Place the word to be spelled in the student's visual recall area. Be sure that the word is written clearly and in good contrast to the background it's on. The student looks at word (externally) and then images it in his mind's eye. Repeat this process until the word flashes completely to mind.

STEP 4: The student should now spell the word forward and backward in his mind's eye. When he can do this easily, continue with Step 5.

STEP 5: Ask the student: "If your best friend came into the room, would you recognize him? What feeling is that (the feeling of recognition)?" The student then looks at word again. Continue cycling between processes until the visually remembered words are familiar.

STEP 6: Tell the student: "From now on, whenever you want to spell a word, simply look up at your picture for it and copy it down."

Andreas and Andreas (1989) point out that for languages that are spelled phonetically like Spanish or German, it would be possible to use an auditory spelling strategy. But for languages like English, this auditory spelling strategy cannot be successfully applied. They quote an old joke:

"How do you spell 'fish' phonetically? The answer is 'ghoti'—*gh* as in enough, *o* as in women, and *ti* as in motion (pp. 11-12)." Consequently, just teach one visual spelling strategy for all languages and the problem is solved.

VOCABULARY

Hager (1990, 1993b) found a similar process for learning vocabulary in a foreign/second language. First elicit a word from a student that she hasn't yet learned. Write it on a colored flashcard in a contrasting different color. Holding up the flashcard to your left (your student's right), say the word in English with the German equivalent; this way the student is familiar with the meaning in English. You then have the student visualize a picture or a "movie" for the word. For instance, the word in English could be "throw." So the student visualizes a person throwing something. After the student has a picture or a movie, have her think of it in as many bright colors as possible, as clearly as possible, as large as possible and so on. (See SUB-MODALITIES.) In doing so, you are accessing as many different submodality distinctions as possible and therefore intensifying the experience. Once the student has constructed a picture for the word, have her write the word "throw" in some crazy manner in the picture. This way she also knows how the word is spelled as well as its meaning. For those learners who have to have everything in black and white, it is possible the learner put a black or white frame around her picture (suggested by June Jackson, personal communication). Naturally this is done in the learner's visual construct area.

Once the student has her picture, move the flashcard down so that it is level and in her construct auditory area. The student is then instructed to imagine a sound that is appropriate for the word. Next move the flashcard down to her kinesthetic area and tell her to imagine an appropriate feeling or feelings to go along with the picture and sounds for the word. Finally, take away the flashcard and tell the learner to again visualize her picture with all her sounds and feelings that go along with the picture of the word.

To double check that the word is stored in memory, hold the flashcard up to your right (his left) for retrieval of the stored word and images and ask what the word means.

After doing this process with several words, have the learner imagine herself in the future at home or wherever she normally learns vocabulary. Here she visualizes herself in the process of using this method, paying attention to sights, sounds, and feelings in her image of herself using this process. Also have the learner imagine how easy and how much fun it is to use the method in this state. Before the student leaves, give her the option of using this method or her old way of learning vocabulary.

This process is very beneficial for a kinesthetic learner who still has not learned how to visually store and retrieve material. Depending on what kind of learner you are working with, parts of this process can be unnecessary. For those learners who are visual, the auditory and kinesthetic parts can be superfluous, and for the auditory learner, the kinesthetic parts can be secondary.

One great advantage to this method is that from the very beginning, the learner has the chance to think in the second/foreign language. As long as the learner is able to imagine pictures, sounds, and feelings for words in the foreign/second language, he will think of only the target language with his images. Once the learner is well versed in the use of this strategy, pictures, sounds and feelings will come to him easily.

READING COMPREHENSION

Often in language teaching, a learner can read something but not know what she has just finished reading. This can be due to the lack of necessary vocabulary or poor contextual analysis skills.

The problem can be observed if you "track" the retrieval strategy of these learners in response to comprehension questions. You can consistently see a pattern of the students attempting to access sound (eye movement side to side). The learner tries to store an auditory sequence and hasn't transferred it into pictures in his mind.

In order to be able to successfully store material, the student first wants to be in a position stimulating for visual processing. Janet Goodrich states, "to maintain the maximum flow of visual energy through your body and to keep both sides of your brain turned on, it is essential to keep your body channels open. Sitting to read is preferable to lying down. The latter can cramp the neck and restrict energy flow up the spine into the visual centers" (see Fig.1.1).

Figure 1.1: Visual Processing Position

As Galyean points out, "a picture is worth a thousand words." "By creating mental pictures and focusing clearly on them, we are actually seeing more of the information coming to us; for example, while reading, it is helpful to create mental pictures of what is being read so we can comprehend more deeply the material presented in the reading" (p. 20).

When the student reads, he should look up over the edge of his book, for example, to store pictures (or, better, a movie) for the material he has just read. By doing this, he is correctly positioning his eyes in the visual area (See Fig. 1: Eye Movement Patterns) for more efficient storage of the read material. This can be done for several sentences at first and then expanded to paragraphs and pages of material. This part can be done alone or in class.

The teacher should ask the student: "What do you remember from what you have read?" Note which sensory modality is used. Then overlap from the used sensory modality to the underused one(s): "You see a beautiful river, the water and the plants. What does the flowing water sound like? What else can you hear? How would the water feel if you walked in it? What else do you feel at the river?"

The teacher can increase the "vitality" of each sensory modality by asking about the qualities of the image, sounds, sensations or feelings (see SUB-MODALITIES). Finally, the teacher should encourage the student to watch her movie and do any necessary editing.

To increase your students' retention of the material, have them draw pictures to represent their feelings about the material or to represent how they might perceive it auditorily.

SUB-MODALITIES

In the beginning of NLP, the structure of meaning was found to occur in the specific sequence of representational systems a person implemented to process information. These sequences were called strategies (see LEARNING STRATEGIES).

It was later found that the intensity of meaning is directly related to sub-modalities, or the component elements, of a given representational system. For example, when you remember a pleasant experience, the intensity of your remembered experience is directly related to the color, size, brightness, and distance of the visual image from you in your mind's eye (Bandler and MacDonald).

The following table shows various aspects of sub-modalities for the three representational systems with which we have been working:

VISUAL	AUDITORY	KINESTHETIC
movie/picture	volume	temperature
size	pitch	movement
shapes/forms	number of sounds	taste
perspective	rhythm	pressure
texture	smell	emotions

Table 1: Sub-modalities

These various distinctions of sub-modalities can be elicited through different questions to establish how the student is processing the material. A few of those that Bandler and MacDonald suggest are the following:

VISUAL   **QUESTIONS**
color/   Is it color or black and white?
black & white
brightness   Are the colors vivid or washed out?
              In that context, is it brighter or darker
              than normal?

AUDITORY
location   Do you hear it from the inside or outside?
mono/stereo   Do you hear it on one side, both sides, or
              is the sound all around you?

KINESTHETIC
quality   How would you describe the body sensation:
              tingling, warm, cold, relaxed, tense, knotted?
location   Where do you feel it in your body?
movement   Is there movement in the sensation?

In the following chapters, we will see how the use of sub-modalities is of great importance in constructing and presenting guided imagery.

CHAPTER 2
"As If . . ."

Those people who have difficulties knowing what they want or are not able to set goals can implement a strategy called "As If" (Laborde, 1988). Syer and Connolly state that this is like "performing 'as if' you were someone or something else which represents a quality that you want to emphasize in your performance" (p. 64).

This strategy can be used in the foreign language classroom to allow the student the chance to really get a picture, sound, or feeling for the language. In this case, the desired "quality" is to be able to speak and perform in the target language.

Syer and Connolly go on to explain how they used this technique with athletes they were working with. They refer to this as "as if . . ." discussions. Everyone on the team imagined that they were someone within their particular sport area. The players then divided into groups of four and spent approximately ten minutes discussing their own strengths and weaknesses with the group as if they were the person they admired but talking about themselves in the third person. An essential part of this "discussion" is that the coach must set a scene for the players (students) before they begin (for example, they might be in the club-house). It is the coach's responsibility to be sure that each group acts out a conversation as if they were really their admired (or selected) person.

Given the chance, the learner can take on new qualities or even perhaps call forth these "new" qualities from his subpersonality. Whitmore refers to this as **creative play.** By acting "as if," we are able to put on a new mask (see ARTWORK) or take it off at will. Whitmore states that this putting on and taking off of a mask is "providing the experience of both being it and having the power not to be it, as well as being **more** than it" (p. 121).

Whitmore also believes that an effective and playful manner in which to work with this quality/qualities (she refers to subpersonality) is to give it a name. Naming it embodies it with more life and definition— it can be like making a new friend. She also believes that "children and adults often enjoy playing the game of naming their subpersonalities and presenting them to others" (p. 117).

Spolin maintains that "the effects of game playing are not only social and cognitive. When players are deeply focused on a game, they are capable of transforming objects or creating them. Whole environments arise spontaneously out of thin air" (p. 4).

When utilizing this strategy, I find that it can be very advantageous to provide a new setting in which the students can acquire the new language. For example, a setting could be a conference for intercultural differences where your students are the conference participants and you are the facilitator. Of course, you do not inform your students of the "as if" strategy, but, as the facilitator, you introduce the setting and provide your students with the needed material so they can take part in the conference. Naturally, the level of your students will make a difference to what extent you are able to carry through the setting.

In order to establish the setting properly, it is also a good idea to work with different kinds of posters and pictures. For example, when I use the theme "A Conference on Intercultural Differences," it normally takes place at Somewhere, USA. Consequently, it is appropriate to have various posters or pictures of the United States to use as anchors and help set the atmosphere (see ANCHORING).

Each day, if it's an intensive course, I always have a greeting waiting for the participants when they come into the room in the morning and after lunch (see Fig. 2.1). This provides them with more stimulus to enjoy and relax during the "conference."

Your conference can start just like any other trip or tour would. The participants are sitting in a semi-circle. The facilitator is standing at the

Life is like a beautiful old tree.
It's magnificent. So take a moment and enjoy it!

Figure 2.1: Greeting

open end of the circle closing it. He greets the participants and introduces himself and the setting.

Of course, the facilitator must know who the participants are. I usually have a roll of toilet paper with names written on it. (This usually gets a good laugh and sets the atmosphere for a light, relaxed "conference.") I then find out from the participants who is who. Of course, with absolute beginners this has to be simplified. (Charles Schmid and Lynn Dhority both have a very good procedure for starting a course with absolute beginners.) During this time, find out as much as possible about each participant (see META-MODEL), giving them the time to develop a new identity. Be flexible enough to allow your participants time enough to develop and imagine this about themselves (their new fictitious selves). To do this, I always tell something about myself. Often what I say is so outlandish that it is obvious to everyone that it can't be possible. The participants catch on very quickly that they too are to let their imaginations go wild and do and act "as if ..." they were someone else. Asking questions also provides needed "new" information about them. However, it is not only the facilitator's job to ask questions—the participants should be free to do so as well. They should have the feeling that this is their trip/tour, and they can ask questions anytime they would like. Spolin maintains that "... a player can only take chances when he or she trusts the games, the group, the sidecoach" (she refers to the teacher as sidecoach) (p. 6).

Once you have established who everyone is, it is good to have them reinforce their identities by filling out I.D. cards for the conference (see Fig. 2.2). The I.D. card should require information you've already obtained such as NAME, PLACE OF BIRTH, etc. After everyone has completed the information, the facilitator collects the I.D.'s and gives one to each participant, but never giving the participant his own. Once everyone has an I.D., the participant draws a picture of the person named on the card. In all exercises, I feel it extremely important that the facilitator always participate. This way he gives the participants the feeling that he is one of the group and not just facilitating, even though he is facilitating their learning of the target language.

Through my experience, I have found that advanced students as well as beginners enjoy the chance to become someone else. Participants have said it is easier for them to be someone else and the fictitious person makes the mistakes, not them.

To make this even more outlandish I often introduce my friend Benny from South Africa or Rainy from Canada. Benny is a hippo hand puppet, and Rainy is a reindeer. Most participants really enjoy having the chance to talk to them and find out about them and their families.

Throughout the whole course you as the facilitator must always be "there" mentally to keep the participants within the realm of the conference. In the beginning, some participants might have to be reminded of their new identity. You want the participants to really become their fictitious person during the course, so much so that it is automatic to react as that new person. You really want your participants to play the "as if..." role—and through your actions, you can make this very clear. If a participant does stray, gently bring him back to his new role.

At the end of a course using the "as if..." strategy, it is always necessary to bring both "persons" or personalities together (bring together the real

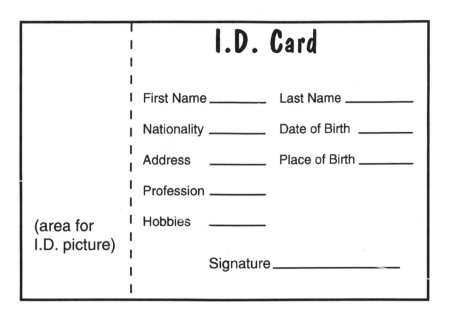

Figure 2.2: I.D. Card

person and fictitious one so that both can integrate into one for later use). In NLP this is referred to as collapsing anchors.

This can be done through visualization where you have each student imagine the one person in her left hand, for example, and the other in her right. Slowly the student brings her hands together and then places them on her chest for total integration. If for some reason a student doesn't want to do this process of collapsing anchors, don't force her. She surely has good reason of her own for not wanting to go through the process.

Laborde (1987) points out that the use of "as if . . ." is much more successful for business people when they project themselves into the future and look back at their success and follow their progress from the past to their future stand point.

This too is possible within the language classroom. At the end of a course, have your students reflect back on what has been done and what they have accomplished during the course. By doing so you provide your students the chance to have the feeling of real accomplishment. However, I would do this after you've collapsed anchors on their fictitious and real person; otherwise it is possible that a student may feel that his accomplishments were not his but those of the fictitious person.

After completing this, have your students individually decide what was their best accomplishment during the course. This doesn't have to be only language—it could, for example, be overcoming a learning barrier. Once they've provided their point, they can draw a picture for it, making it true to life or abstract. After this have each student show his or her picture and tell about it. Of course, if the learner doesn't want to share this with the others, he or she should not be forced to.

CHAPTER 3
Guided Imagery

Throughout our history, storytelling has been one vital means of communicating information and ideas. Jacobsen (1983) states that "a good storyteller involves his listener. His voice becomes a symphony. His expressions and movements paint the most vivid of scenes. His words delve down to the deepest levels of feeling, leaving a taste of experience not soon to be forgotten" (p. 114).

Moore believes there is an intimate connection between stories and dreams. When listening to a story, the listener is in the same state as when dreaming at night. Moore states ". . . storytelling reaches beyond the surface of normal waking consciousness, delving into the area we visit when we dream at night. So storytelling presents itself as an ancient technique for experiencing the dreaming state while we are awake" (p. 71).

This beautiful experience is also possible in the foreign language class. In the above quote, Jacobsen was referring to storytelling but within the realm of using it to expedite a learner's progress in the form of visualization. This technique is referred to by different names: guided imagery (Schmid), visualization (Bry), fantasy trips (Jacobsen) and mental rehearsal (Syer and Connolly). No matter what the name, the effect is the same.

In using fantasy trips, it is possible to anchor good and positive experiences (imagined or past) in order to: 1) teach the material to be learned, 2) review material already learned, or 3) relax and turn off events that have happened before coming to class.

The function of visualization can be of great value for learners who have worked all day and cannot so easily turn off the previous task. A fantasy trip gives them the opportunity to focus on something other than their previous work while providing them the chance to let it all go before they start learning a language.

As Charles Schmid (p. 19) points out, there are three different kinds of guided imagery: **guided, semi-guided** and **unguided.** Guided is when the instructor fills in the details of what, when, where, and how. Semi-guided is when the students are given the location but are allowed to fill in the details for themselves. And an unguided trip is when the students are allowed to go wherever they want, when they want, how they want, and to see or experience what they want. In most classrooms, I believe guided visualizations are more prevalent, but the other methods can also be of great help when implemented in a creative way.

In constructing a fantasy trip, it's important to remember these steps:

STEP 1: For what purpose are you writing a guided fantasy? For one of the above mentioned reasons or a combination of several? To get started, think of a setting. Settings may be walking along the beach, walking through a forest or park, sitting in a large field of flowers, and so on.

STEP 2: List the things you would see, hear, feel, taste, and smell in your particular setting. If you chose the beach, your list might look something similar to this.

SEE	HEAR	FEEL	TASTE/SMELL
blue water	waves	cool water	salty air
white fluffy	walking in	warm breeze	favorite drink
clouds	water	sand between	
white sand	wind in	toes	
bright sun	your hair		

When you write or construct your fantasy trip, be sure to include as many different VAK elements as possible. Syer and Connolly emphasize that "it is important to remember that visualization includes an auditory and a kinesthetic (feeling) component. In other words, if you visualize yourself moving, you may see, hear, and feel yourself moving. In most visualization, the kinesthetic sense is particularly important" (p. 47).

Everyone has a preference for one sensory mode, and if you leave one out, you could be leaving out the one someone else really needs in order to be able to follow you. Syer and Connolly state, "The stranger the sensory component and the more realistic the visualization, the more powerful the message to your nervous system. The more powerful the message, the more effective the mental rehearsal will be in organizing your nervous system to respond during your sports performance" (p. 54)—or, for our purpose, language performance.

According to Thomas Armstrong (1987), teaching that disregards feelings of any kind and focuses solely on rational learning (visual and/ or auditory) fails to acknowledge the fact that there is a normal balance in life between feeling and thinking. This disregard can seriously damage any chance of real learning taking place.

If you want to give your beginners the chance to experience a review of their material by experiencing it internally, you can do a mini-fantasy trip with them. Just as before, have your students relax and just listen to what you recite. They shouldn't really physically do what you say, only imagine doing it.

If you want to cover a special item in your guided imagery, i. e. forms of irregular verbs, you must decide what, where, and how and when in the trip to implement it. Keep in mind that creating your visualization in the present tense makes the visualization more vivid.

Syer and Connolly also point out that while doing visualization, some people watch themselves acting from a slight distance, while others feel themselves acting from inside looking out (in NLP terms, this is associated and dissociated). They go on to claim that if you watch yourself looking out, you are probably more kinesthetically oriented, and if you are outside yourself observing yourself, you are probably more visually oriented.

Galyean states that "watching images pass through us is like watching a movie." We can do two things:

1. Remain detached like an objective or outside observer, and see the images as separate from us.

2. Become one with (or merge with) the images and let ourselves act as the image. We can actually feel the images in our body" (p. 29).

Being aware of this distinction makes it easier for the teacher to understand why both techniques need to be included in the guided imagery.

Another thing to remember is to use affirmations throughout your fantasy trip. Davis et al. suggest using positive statements that affirm your ability to relax. Syer and Connolly state that "some affirmations are doubly effective because of their vivid language" (p. 86). This can be very skillfully implemented in guided imagery to help people relax, but I feel it is also valuable in affirming the learner's ability to learn a language easily and well. This can be essential for those learners who have learning barriers. In various parts or in a particular part of your fantasy trip, it is possible to build in a phrase like "English is so simple to understand," or "speaking English is so enjoyable," etc. I build the phrase in toward the end of a fantasy trip—the students have experienced a fantasy trip already in English and understood at least in general what they were to do during the trip, so they really notice that it is simple to understand.

STEP 3: Before starting your fantasy trip, you want to give your students the chance to physically relax. Syer and Connolly claim that both relaxation and concentration are needed to visualize successfully.

STEP 4: Have participants sit or lie down in a comfortable place. My experience has proven that sitting is better than lying—sitting reduces the chances of falling asleep. Be sure that hands or legs are not crossed— this way the energy in the students' bodies can circulate freely.

STEP 5: Present your fantasy trip in a soft, soothing voice. Be sure you speak as clearly as possible and that your background music or sounds are not too loud. You want your students to hear you. Give your presentation slowly but not so slowly that you lose momentum. After each new suggestion, pause to allow your students time to do what you've suggested (Williams).

STEP 6: Bring your students back to the place where they started in their fantasy and give them a few seconds to arrive at this place before asking them to move their feet, legs, arms, and hands and to open their eyes.

STEP 7: Ask questions about the trip using VAK distinctions, or do various activities to intensify the guided imagery experience.

Galyean points out that "expressing and communicating are ways of imprinting (not forgetting) the information in our memories. It helps to follow imagery work with a verbal and/or nonverbal mode of expressing what we've experienced. We find that drawing, painting, writing poems, dancing, moving, singing, chanting, sculpting, building, as well as talking about and writing are quite good ways of helping us to remember and learn from our imagery work. Often a fuller understanding of our images comes while we are expressing our experiences in one or a combination of these modes" (pp. 29-30). See Figure 3.1 for an overview.

If you are unsure that a particular learner is able to see any pictures, or that your class is ready to try visualization, there are some simple exercises to do with them. Take something that is very familiar to the learners, such as an apple. Have your students close their eyes and imagine an apple. Throughout this exercise you must remember to include as many different sub-modality distinctions as possible (see SUB-MODALITIES). For example, your students should imagine what color the apple is, how big it is, whether the picture is clear or not so clear, how the apple feels, how it smells or tastes, where the apple is—on a table, on the floor, etc.—how it sounds when they bite into the apple, etc. Initially, this could be difficult for some students, but with practice it becomes easier and easier. (For more suggestions on exercises you can do, see Michael Grinder.) If this is too simple, progress to the next level of guided imagery.

When guided imagery is used in the classroom, its effect depends a great deal on its function during that particular lesson. If I'm using it for relaxation or "turn-off" purposes, I always start with it. However, it can also be used to review previous material or introduce new. This can take place during the same fantasy trip you use for relaxation at the beginning of the lesson or later on, but I would not recommend doing more than one guided trip during a lesson.

Guided imagery can be of great help when reviewing material that students have just learned. For example, when working with beginners, it's more likely than not that you won't be able to do a complete fantasy trip in the foreign language because of your students' lack of understanding of the needed language. So I find it a very nice close to the lesson to do a mini-fantasy trip to review what we've just covered in the lesson. If you've just covered introduction phrases in class, have your students relax in their chairs, close their eyes, and just imagine the sentences you recite. Here's an example.

Hi, my name is Peter, what's your name?
(In a little different voice, perhaps deeper) Hi, my name is John. Where are you from, Peter?
Oh, I'm from Denver, Colorado, and you?
(Deeper voice) I'm from Texas.

Make sure you allow your students enough time so they can imagine what you're saying. Of course, you don't want to use any questions or answers your students haven't learned. A sequence of actions that you could have your students mentally image could be as follows:

1. Stand up.   *6. Close the door.*
2. Sit down.   *7. Walk to your table.*
3. Stand up.   *8. Turn around.*
4. Walk to the door.   *9. Sit down.*
5. Open the door.

Some will be able to visualize themselves doing the commands you give, while others will only be able to feel the action. As Syer and

Purpose of Guided Imagery

1. To teach the upcoming material
2. To review already learned material
3. To relax and turn off events that have happened before coming to class.

Types of Guided Imagery

Guided   Semi-guided   Unguided

Steps For Constructing Guided Imagery

1. For what purpose are you writing a guided fantasy?
2. List the things you would see, hear, feel, taste and smell in your particular setting.
3. Include various kinds of affirmations.
4. Before starting your fantasy journey, you want to give your students the chance to physically relax.
5. Have students sit or lie down in a comfortable position. Be sure that hands or legs are not crossed—this way the energy in the students' bodies can circulate freely.
6. Present your fantasy journey in a soft and soothing voice using a visual posture to help visual quality of your voice. Speak clearly and keep any background music softer than your voice. Present slowly and leave pauses between suggestions or word clusters.
7. Bring your students back to the place where they started in their fantasy and give them a few seconds to arrive at this place before telling them to move their feet, legs, arms and hands and open their eyes.
8. Ask questions about trip using VAK distinctions or do various activities to intensify the guided imagery experience.

Figure 3.1: Overview of Guided Imagery

Connolly point out, this mental feeling of movement is just as good as the real thing. Through research done on athletes, it has been found that our muscles react to imagined physical training in the same manner as when we physically move our muscles. So by reviewing or learning in this way, we are providing our students the chance to fully internalize the material. If nothing more, your students have a moment at the end of the lesson to relax and let everything sink in.

With beginners, it is better to have them visualize someone else doing whatever is happening in the fantasy trip or have them feel what they're doing because for many it's difficult to visualize themselves without some practice. And feeling what you're doing is much easier because you're still associated.

It is possible you will run into some learners who cannot visualize pictures. Explain to them that it's no problem, that the pictures come with practice (see above). Also make clear to the fantasy trip beginner that he shouldn't try to force himself into seeing, hearing, or feeling the images. If he does this, he's only producing the negative effect of stress and strain that we want to overcome in learning. He should just relax and let come what may. If he doesn't consciously pick up what's being covered, he will subconsciously, and this is where most of our learning takes place anyway (Rose). Murphy points out that 90% of our mental life is subconscious during normal waking hours.

A good source for ideas on fantasy trips is De Mille's *Put Your Mother On The Ceiling*. In his book, he presents various guided imageries for children, but they can be used for adults, too.

For much more advanced students, I find that visualization provides a good chance to review and intensify previously covered grammatical points. I like to do a guided imagery "on the beach" with my students to relax and review the present participles of irregular verbs. A cassette with sounds of the ocean helps to enhance the experience.

When the students are relaxed, I guide them along the beach, enjoying everything they see, hear, and feel. I have them reach a point on the beach and say:

You slowly start to walk again and see in front of you a beautiful stick laying on the ground.

You slowly reach down and pick it up and feel how good it feels in your hand.

With this stick you start to write words in the wet sand. Perhaps you write . . .

> *read read read   put put put*
> *write wrote written   drink drank drunk*
> *see saw seen   drive drove driven*
> *hide hid hidden   come came come*
> *eat ate eaten   go went gone*

You now stand for a moment and look at your work and feel so very good. As you stand and watch, you hear the sound of the waves coming in and you see the waves coming in and slowly washing away your words, so very slowly.

You feel so happy inside because you know the words. It's so beautiful watching the waves. So relaxing, So very relaxing.

To finish the guided imagery, I take them back along the way they came, at which time they still enjoy all the sights, sounds, and feelings they've experienced on this beautiful beach. This does not have to take place at the beach—it could be in a meadow, and the students write the words in the tall grass or watch an airplane write the words in the sky with the smoke from the exhaust. After your students have arrived back, ask them questions about their experience such as:

Have you ever been to this beach before?
Have you ever watched the birds fly so freely over the beach?
How did you feel?
What would you do the next time on the beach?
Were you there alone? Who was with you?
How did you feel listening to the birds?
How did you feel when your words were washed away?

You can have your students draw pictures about their beach trip, their feelings on the beach (abstract or real), or the sounds they heard. Here you must be careful, because many people won't have sounds or feelings or perhaps not even pictures (one of the three is sure but perhaps not all of them). Give them options. You can also have them write a story or poem about their beach or experience on the beach.

To reinforce the irregular verbs from the fantasy trip, pantomime can be used. Have one student take a card from many. On the card are three irregular verbs that you have already worked on in class. The student then pantomimes a sketch for the three words on the card. Once she has finished, the teacher asks, "What has she just done?" eliciting the correct forms for the verbs pantomimed.

In her book, *Thinking, Changing, Rearranging,* Jill Anderson presents a good exercise for dealing with feelings which can be applied here. Have your students pick two or three different feelings they had during their fantasy trip, and with a partner, combine their different feelings into a role play. After everyone has presented their play, talk about how this might relate to the fantasy trip. Of course, you may have to be a fast thinker to find some way the role play may be related emotionally or on a feeling basis to the guided imagery, but more often than not this is not a difficult task. By doing this, the learner also has the chance to learn vocabulary for feelings and emotions which the normal foreign/second language learner does not have, and of course, to learn how to express this correctly. (For more ideas see Hager, 1989.)

Guided imageries can also be used for English for Special Purposes. In technical English courses, I like to do a visualization in a temple (background music *Silk Road* by Kitaro) (Hager 1993a). Once the students have entered the temple, they look around and see, feel, and hear what they may. After they have had time to do this, I guide them to the middle of the temple where they see a small table. On this small table they see a machine (of their choice). They watch how it works, listen to it working, and perhaps touch it as it is working. Slowly I have them leave the temple, taking with them all their good pictures, sounds, and feelings.

Once they've "returned" to their seats, I have them draw a picture of their machine while thinking about how they can explain what it is and how it works. (I go on the same "trip" as my students while telling it and also draw a picture for my machine.) After a student has explained his machine, the others have the chance to ask questions. Once this part has been completed, I summarize what they have drawn and shown by explaining how one machine perhaps powers another or is important in some way for the use of the other ones. That way all pictures and experiences within the group are connected into one communal experience.

The use of guided imagery can also help students practice seeing themselves doing something that might be difficult for them, but which is simple in the fantasy. You can do anything in fantasy. Ristad found when she did simple guided imageries with her piano students, it made it easier for them to do in reality what they had just done in their fantasy. O'Connor points out that even our body partakes in this activity. It has been found that muscle activity in mental rehearsal corresponds closely to the mood of the music used.

Jensen points out that there are two important points to remember about guiding an imagery. First, ask your students to give you a sign so you know they are following you. He continues by saying that although some students may not signal, continue your imagery, providing more sensory stimulation until your students find that moment from the past. His second point is to be sure you create an "anchor" for the experience, i. e., a special tone of voice, a song, or gesture such as hand on knees (pp. 91-92).

I feel Jensen's idea for signalling to indicate whether the student is following is sometimes appropriate for groups you don't know. With new groups, it is a good idea not to go on the fantasy trip with them. If you use VAK appropriately while presenting your imagery to a new group, it is really not necessary to have a signal from them, because you already know if your students are following. For example, while presenting your trip you can talk about eating or drinking in your guided imagery, and you can observe that the students move their lips or adam's apple as if they were eating or drinking. This, of course, indicates they are with you. And if they are not with you, it is not so tragic. Perhaps for reasons unknown to you, a student may need this quiet moment for himself to just relax.

Jensen's idea to use anchors is a good one—and you can also format the experience so that the student has complete mental control over it. When I do a guided imagery, I normally give the student the option to come back to her starting place/situation any time she wants (for example, we are on the beach and have just turned around to go back to where we started on the beach).

> *... on your way back to the point where you started you are still enjoying everything you've seen, heard, felt, smelled or tasted. All these beautiful things you take with you. Whenever you want or need you can just return and enjoy this beautiful place. Just think of this fantastic beach and enjoy the effects.*

CHAPTER 4
Timelines

Conceptualizing the use of different tenses in a foreign language can be trying and frustrating for the foreign language learner. She can only apply the different forms for the different tenses(s) in the foreign language once she has internalized the concept of these tense(s). These could easily be different from those in her mother tongue, or at least the use of the forms to indicate the different tenses.

In NLP, it has been found that each individual has his own way of sorting and organizing time. This important concept is referred to as timeline. Steve and Connirae Andreas (1987) state that the location of time for each individual is important for keeping track of reality. Through their work, the Andreases have found that every individual lines up his experiences on a continuum in relation to his physical being. Some may locate the past to their left, others behind them, and still others to their right—some people locate their future to their right, others to their left, and others in front of them. The distance of the location of the experience in relation to the person depends on the occurrence of the experience. Normally the farther back in time or the farther into the future the experience was or will be puts it farther away from the central point of the line (the person). The Andreases (1987) say that for most people, "the past is usually a line off to the left, the present right in front of you, and the future in a line to the right" (p. 8). They also maintain that "the timeline is usually aligned with the person's accessing cues. People almost always have their past on the same side that they have visual memory, and their future is on the same side as visual construct" (1987, p. 6).

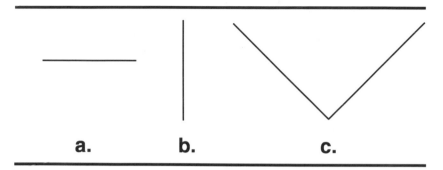

Figure 4.1: Types of personal timelines

Hager (1990) states that a timeline can usually have three standard forms. Those people who have Timeline A usually have this line situated just a little in front of them. In most situations, these people are disassociated in relation to their timeline. Timeline B usually goes directly through the person—the person is its middle point. Thus the person is associated to his timeline. Timeline C people are often located at the point of the "V," either being associated or disassociated.

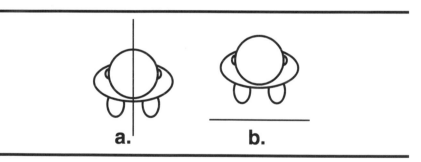

Figure 4.2: Associated (a) and Disassociated (b) timelines

Timelines can either be associated or disassociated (see Fig. 4.2) and can vary from situation to situation. In English, for example, the normal form is like Fig. 4.2b for native speakers of English (Andreas et al., 1987).

This knowledge is of great importance for language teachers, because we use our instinct when we gesture with our hand, for example, to demonstrate some action in the past—more than likely always to our left. Being aware of the concept of timelines, we can assume that most learners will need us to demonstrate on our right (*their* left) so it fits into their timeline setup. This holds true when we are demonstrating grammatical rules, for example. But when we are relating to our students something from our own past, it is not necessary for us to translate this for our students and their timeline. They are able to do this for themselves; it happens every day in normal conversation.

Those students who have another timeline setup (not the standard form Fig. 4.1a) don't need to be left out. You can do a simple exercise with your students to discover their timeline. Form groups of twos or threes and have one student tell another to think about an activity that she does every day, such as brushing his teeth. The third student and the student giving instructions observe the responding student's actions. Instructions that can be given are:

1. Think about a time when you brushed your teeth a long time ago—perhaps five years ago.
2. Now think about having brushed your teeth a week ago.
3. Think about brushing your teeth now.
4. Think about brushing your teeth next week.
5. Think about brushing your teeth five years from now.

The two observing students watch for changes in location of eyes, hands, or other indicators to show where the third student is perceiving each point in time. The student giving instructions can then ask the third where she perceived each point in time. This can be done for each person in the group. Every student then must remember where she perceived the different times. This way both you and the student know whether her past was to the left, in back of her or to her right, present in front of her and future to the right, in front or to her left. If you get results that aren't in a line continuum, don't panic; there are people who vary from the norm. The most important thing for you to know is where their past, present, and future are located.

Having information about timelines, VAK, and anchoring, you are ready to teach verb tenses that are difficult for students to understand. Because almost all learners of English as a foreign/second language have difficulties with the present continuous, let's start with it. We know that on our timeline, the present is located directly in front of us, so we want to implement this in teaching the present continuous tense.

Have your students stand up and walk in place; while doing this, they can check all their VAK input. The teacher does this with the students and says "I'm walking." Now have your students stop and step back so the place where they "were walking" is directly in front of them. Standing there, have your students watch themselves walking on this spot in front of them. Have them feel the experience of walking on this spot and listen to what it sounds like walking on this spot. For some, it could be difficult initially to be able to visualize themselves walking, and adding the other VAK modes provides possibilities for everyone to take part in the experience. (See VISUALIZATION for Syer and Connolly's comment about some not being able to visualize themselves but able to feel). While the students are in their trance state, you again say "I'm walking." In this way, you anchor the auditory "I'm walking" with the visual and kinesthetic aspects of watching and feeling themselves walk. By being in this trance state, you facilitate the students' learning of this concept with the correct forms. Because this goes quickly, I often do several different verbs one after another, using verbs that are easily done in the classroom; walking, writing, reading, sitting, etc.

For students who haven't had much experience with visualization, the visual part of this exercise can be difficult. Some of my students have asked if it's bad when they can't visualize themselves doing an activity. I tell them that it's easy for some to visualize and easy for others to feel the activity. Their response has confirmed this. I must, however, point out that for beginners most of this exercise must be done in the learner's native language. Such exercises are only possible in the target language for more advanced students.

This kind of exercise is also possible for the Present Perfect in English. To commence, designate one area in the classroom for the past and one for the present. It is important to designate two places in front of the class: the place for the past should be on your right (the class's left) and the place for the present on your left (the class's right). Later, when you want to refer to the past, present perfect or present, just indicate the appropriate area, perhaps with a hand gesture. The area is already anchored on the appropriate side or place of the student's timeline, which triggers the appropriate reaction in the student (referring to the concept of time).

Once you have the appropriate places for the present and the past, have your students stand up and walk with you from the past (starting in the right place) to the present. You must have your students start walking so that the past on their timeline is located in the right place on their timeline. For example, if your student's past on his timeline is behind him, he must walk to the present with the past behind him. If his past is on his left, he can walk sideways so that the past location remains on his left. The person with the past on his right can walk sideways so the past is on his right. If you don't know your students' exact timeline, have everyone walk sideways so the past is on their left. This way you'll be placing most of your students in the right position. While this is being done, the students are checking their pictures, sounds, and feelings in the past, then moving from the past to the present. Being in the present time (and correct place in the classroom), you have your student look back at themselves in the past to the present or feel their way from the past to the present. Again the students check their pictures, sounds, and feelings during this experience (Hager, 1989).

On completion of this, say to your students, "You have walked from the past to the present." Here you explain to your students the use of the present perfect while referring (gesturing) to the different places (anchors) in the room and to their walk from one place to the other. This exercise can be easily done for all different tenses.

Connirae and Steve Andreas (1989) point out that "every language has some way to express time—the awareness of past, present or future. In some cultures, time is thought of as a series of cycles: birth, death, rebirth, etc. In English, time is often thought of as a 'line' and many of us learned history out of books that had diagrams of events occurring in a line across the page" (p. 191).

Once my learners have reached the present perfect tense, I explain to them what a timeline is. I start by presenting a straight line, explaining it as a line in time. Then I explain to them how in history books (for English speaking cultures) this line is used.

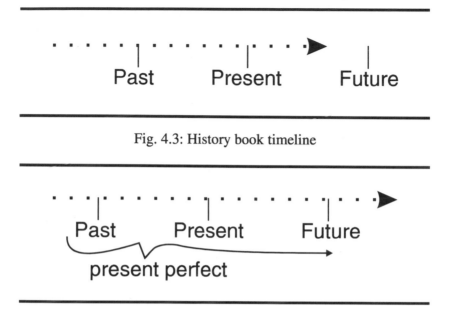

Fig. 4.3: History book timeline

Fig. 4.4: Timeline with present perfect

Then I go on to explain how the present perfect fits into this time line. Until my students reach the present perfect, I don't explain the timeline concept to them. I simply do relaxing exercises to instill the present continuous, future, and past without their knowledge of the concept behind it.

Through the use of trance state or visualization, it is possible to provide such a line for your learners. Once you have clarified the tense you're teaching, have them relax in their chairs with their eyes closed and imagine a person (man, woman, child; but in the beginning, avoid having them imagine themselves because of the difficulty of doing so). In their mind's eye, the person is doing something right at the moment, such as walking. You can have your students check their VAK at the same time. Once they have done this, have them imagine the person doing the same activity in the future. When this is complete, have your students again imagine the person doing the same activity in the past.

Your students then watch this person in the past and see that he is doing the activity from the past to the present and perhaps on into the future.

Always have your students check their VAK aspects for each step. For example, if you have your students imagine a man walking, you can say, "the man is walking at the moment"; for the past, "the man walked"; for the future, "the man is going to walk"; and for the present perfect, "the man has walked from the past to the present." For each tense, have your students write, in their mind's eye under their picture of the action, for example, "the man has walked from the past to the present."

If you start out with beginners, it is possible to do this as you cover a new tense, each time adding to your students timeline a new tense. Or if you do this after having already completed several tenses, you can construct a timeline up to the tense you are just covering in class. The Andreases (1989) point out that "by imaging these events in different locations, your brain knows whether each one is the past, the present, or the future" (pp. 192-193).

I also find it interesting to talk to my students about the location of their times on their timelines. As of now my students confirm what Steve and Connirae Andreas maintain about the past being on the person's left, the present directly in front of the person, and the future to their right. However, some students felt that the explanation of the timeline itself influenced how they constructed their timeline in English! A couple of students have said that they wanted to have the English timeline in a different arrangement, but because the timeline on the board was the "normal" English timeline, they tried to keep it that way. For this reason, I draw a timeline on the board to show them a normal timeline for a normal right-handed person. When I explain the timeline to my students, I also tell them this fact. This is why it is possible to instill in them an English timeline which could be identical to their own. But those tenses that vary from those in their mother tongue must be emphasized with an activity such as having the students write in their mind's eye at the right location on their timeline a sentence for the tense they are imagining.

By using the timeline, you can give your students another timeline or a variation of their own for the English language. Then they can fill in new tense forms or tenses that their native language may not have or may utilize in another way, like the Present Progressive or the Present Perfect Progressive in English.

CHAPTER 5
New Behavior Generator

In learning a language, the learner is often not able to react or behave like a native speaker of the language. This is due to factors such as not being aware of differences between their native culture and the target one.

Dilts and Green state that "behavior is geared toward adaptation. This has two corollaries: a) individuals make the best choices available to them at any point in time—if given a better choice they will take it; b) underlying every behavior is a positive intent" (1983, p. 19). Both of these behaviors apply to the language learner. The learner is only using the best choice she has, that being perhaps the wrong one for the target language, but the right one for her native culture/language. Because of her good intent to communicate in the only way she has at her disposal at the time, she uses the wrong behavior or strategy in the target culture/language.

Syer and Connolly point out that "with proper training, you can learn correct attitudes and reactions as readily as physical skills. The distraction must be stimulated for two reasons: firstly, so that you may recognize the pattern of your reaction; and secondly, so that you may practice the technique to overcome the distraction" (p. 13). Here they refer to wrong behavior/strategy as distraction.

Whatever it might be called—"wrong behavior," "Positive Structuring," (Sinetar) "Paradigms," (Barker) "distraction," or New Behavior Generator (NBG)—the fact remains that the learner must be given the chance to correct the misuse. Through the use of the following techniques, it is easy for her or him to do so.

CARL A. RUDISILL LIBRARY
LENOIR-RHYNE COLLEGE

Vogel Zanger adeptly points out that ". . . most people are not aware of their own nonverbal communication, because it is so much a part of them; it just feels like the only natural way to act. So to learn about another culture, you must watch carefully how people act and how they react to you" (p. 17). Here too the New Behavior Generator can be of great assistance for any level learner in acquiring such skills.

Cameron-Bandler et al. show how the basics of the NBG can be used with children to help guide them toward attainment of the skills and personal attributes that their parents feel will allow them to enjoy gratifying lives. The basic steps are as follows:

STEP 1: The parents must decide what they want their child to learn. Cameron-Bandler et al. point out that there are two reasons why this is so important: 1) by making these goals explicit, the parents make it possible to evaluate whether these goals are congruent with who the child is as a person; 2) it is important to be aware of the intended goals. This way the parents have explicit outcomes to relate to and move toward in the interactions with their child (pp. 247-248).

STEP 2: The parents should then take time to evaluate the list of goals intended for the child with respect to what is known about him or her as an individual. For example, are the goals congruent with the child or could they be in the future? (p. 248)

STEP 3: Next the parents must specify what kinds of behaviors and responses are indicative of that goal. Once the goal is specified, it is possible for the parents to provide the child with experiences that will assist him or her in learning what is needed for this goal.

STEP 4: Underlying the examples for this "change" is an emphasis on learning as perceived within the range of the future, and the cause/effect relationships that will lead to that future. Here the parents select one goal and imagine their child being able to achieve it in the future (p. 250).

STEP 5: Next the parents must imagine what kinds of learning experiences they could create that will make that future a reality.

Cameron-Bandler et al. point out that "the salient point here is that of generating a learning experience for your child provides a reference experience that will be useful" (p. 252).

STEP 6: The parents need to take the other skills and attributes on their list and process them just as with the first one. It should be noted that the parents have to continually and consistently use this strategy in daily interactions over time—otherwise there is little use in going to the trouble (p. 252).

STEP 7: The last point is to future-pace. The parents imagine themselves responding appropriately and consistently in possible future situations that involve the desired goal (p. 253).

Syer and Connolly maintain there are five steps toward creating change when learning new skills in sports.

1. Recognition
Before changing anything of great substance in your performance, you first must be able to recognize exactly what it is you are doing. They also claim that once you have discovered what you are doing, nine times out of ten, you will be able to see what it is you are doing wrong.

2. Acceptance
Recognizing what you are doing should be accompanied by acceptance of what you are doing before attempting to change. Your present behavior is based on a natural response to the setting that existed at the time while learning that behavior.

3. Coordination
After having recognized the problem and accepting the reasons for it, you are in a good position to make a decision about what behaviors to keep and what to change. Recognition and acceptance will make it possible for you to list the factors needing your attention and to decide on a course to deal with them.

4. Integration
Once you have identified a different and more appropriate response to the problem/situation, you progress to the stage where you integrate the

new response into the total performance. This is accomplished by consciously selecting the new response to the old situation whenever appropriate.

5. Synthesis
The last stage is experiencing the new pattern intertwining perfectly with the rest of your approach and skills. Consequently, some new quality or potential arises and you find yourself reacting in a way which exceeds your previous limitation (pp. 103-104).

Syer and Connolly illustrate this well in a diagram from their book, *Sporting Body Sporting Mind* (p.105).

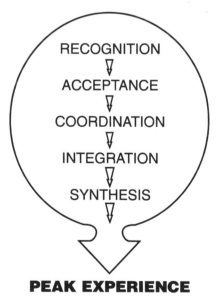

PEAK EXPERIENCE

Figure 5.1: Peak Experience

Through his work with Asian refugees and immigrants learning English as a second language, Charles Faulkner took the idea of the New Behavior Generator to more effectively and creatively teach his students. In his teacher training manual, he suggests the following eight steps for the New Behavior Generator in language learning:

1. Decide which piece of language or behavior you want to be able to do.
2. As you listen to a dialogue, visualize a native speaker model doing it.
3. Step into the image and have the feelings: breathing, rhythms, gestures, emotions, etc.
4. Is it a satisfying experience for you? If yes, go to Step 7. If no, go to Step 5.
5. Step out of the image, and construct an image of yourself doing the language or behavior.
6. Adjust the behavior of the image of yourself so that it is comfortable for you.
7. Step into the image and have the feelings.
8. Experience the whole movie of the piece of language or behavior being in the movie.

Once you have gone through these steps of your movie and have experienced the language/behavior in your movie, test it on a native speaker. If it is up to par, practice it vividly in your mind's eye. By doing so, you will be practicing your success.

If you have made a "mistake" and would like to do it better the next time, watch yourself in your movie up to the point where you make your "mistake." Then change your actions in your movie for your "mistake" so they are as you'd like to have them or you feel they should be. Observe yourself recover from the "mistake" and make the situation better. Once you're satisfied with your movie, again vividly experience being in the new movie.

In a personal communication, Mr. Faulkner elaborated more on his ideas for the use of the New Behavior Generator. He pointed out that it is essential to provide the learner with a new experience while learning a foreign/second language. In doing so, you are breaking the state from the learner's own world/experience to the new experience you are providing. Thus you are creating a new physical as well as a mental state for the language learner. This is exactly what the "as if ..." strategy does (see "AS IF").

He went on to say that the New Behavior Generator has three different stages:

STAGE 1: In Stage 1, the learner does skits, such as waiting for the bus or ordering a hamburger at McDonalds. The teacher (if he is a native speaker or good facsimile) can also have his students mimic him as a model. The students can also act on other people's behalf. For example, a student could imagine that she is a South American now living in the States, and her sister, who doesn't speak English half as well as the student, comes to visit . So the student has to act on behalf of her sister in whatever she does. Here the weaker students should be given the roles which require more speaking and acting.

It's of importance to note that there are three positions involved in learning. The first is yourself, the associated person, the second someone else within the conversation or action, and the third a totally dissociated person. This is referred to as the Perceptual Position Model." It is just like the triad below (Faulkner, personal communication).

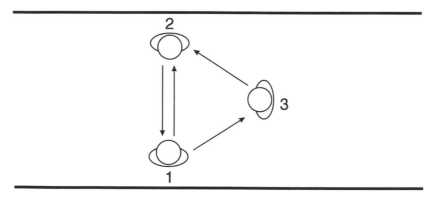

Fig. 5.2.: Perceptual Position Model Triad

In order to get to the third position, one has to go through the first two positions. Sometimes learners are in the third position and stay there through the whole process of learning and acquiring a language. Our task as teachers is to make it possible for the learner to, for example, be in the first position and do something in the second position. We want our learners to be flexible but associated—otherwise the new target language will never become an internal part of them.

The final point to Stage 1 is when the learner starts to learn distinctions. I believe Faulkner means this to be something like Krashen's Monitor Model—not only for grammar but also for physiological and cultural distinctions.

STAGE 2: In Stage 2, the learner needs to find appropriate models and try them on. Bandler points out that a person modelling someone else tries to take the best representation for the way a person does a task and make it available to himself. For example, famous people can be role-played so they function as a model, or the learner can go out on the street and observe what the natives do and use this as an example. In this stage, the learner wants to increase his level of distinctions and his flexibility, as well as changing around the perceptual position model to the sequence 3-2-1 for more flexibility.

STAGE 3: In Stage 3, the learner will be editing her perceptions/movies. During this stage, the learner has to be aware of the fact that she will make mistakes. Here it is possible to provide examples of doing something badly, and how one progresses to proficiency while instilling an internal feeling of whether something has been done well, adequately, or poorly. Once the learner has reached the point of success (after movie editing), she redoes her success five times to reinforce it.

Faulkner also points out that the New Behavior Generator is fifty percent of the teaching/learning experience. He also believes that the NBG helps the learner overcome any beliefs he might have of not being able to learn a new language. He goes on to say that the objective of the NBG is not to master new behavior but a process of step by step refining to get to a target, pointing out that the NBG is a model for physiological change.

NBG in the foreign language classroom can be simple to apply. The teacher first provides the class with a topic of interest and need (using the telephone, waiting for the bus, going to a business meeting, etc.). Then the teacher gives the students the task of presenting a theater skit (this is a term used by John Grinder to refer to role plays)—something such as "Phoning An Operator To Get Information." The students must not only think about and produce a dialogue for the skit but also all the other appropriate physiological aspects for a play (theater sense). Once the students have completed their preparations, they present it. Charles Faulkner (personal communication) believes it is appropriate to only correct inappropriate behavioral or functional uses (for example, physiology or phraseology), and the grammar mistakes will be taken care of by themselves or through the assistance of fellow students. I would like to go one step further and suggest that the teacher should not correct inappropriate behavioral or functional uses directly. This can be done by the students themselves with the help of an audiocassette or videocassette.

I suggest that the students present their skit and then listen to the audiocassette or watch the video dealing with the same problem, idea or situation (in our example, "Phoning The Operator For Information"). Once the students have done this, the teacher helps them find the differences between their presentation(s) and the audiocassette or video. When using an audiocassette it is not possible to watch for differences in physiology, so the teacher must be able to point out these differences to the students. (This is, of course, the great advantage of video.) But if you only have cassettes, you will still be able to find differences in intonation patterns, phraseology or injectors, for example. Once you have viewed or listened to and discussed the differences, have your students go inside themselves and view their original movie of the situation. Then have them change anything in their movie that varies from what you as a group have decided to be appropriate. Your students then view their movie again, this time with the needed changes.

During this process, you want to be sure that your students are checking their internal pictures, sounds, and feelings. By doing this, you intensify and personalize their new experience, allowing it to become more "their" experience. Once this has been done, have your students step into their own movie and enjoy the new and different experience. They should repeat viewing the success four or five times for better internalization.

In the "regular" NBG (see Step 6 of Faulkner's 8 Steps of NBG) one goes inside and feels how it is to be in this new movie/situation, and one changes things until it feels good to be in this movie. However, I have to agree with Charles Faulkner (personal communication) when he points out that this step is inappropriate for language learning. By doing this, the learner will always end up at the original starting point, because this feels natural and good to him. New language situations should feel different, perhaps even weird, because they are new and different. Consequently, this step in the process can be left out.

After you have finished the skit, it is appropriate to provide your students with further cultural information about this situation to give them more background (for example, using the telephone in the United States). Reading and discussing the cultural notes provides good discussion material as well as giving the students the chance to better understand the native speakers.

It is always good to end with guided imagery to give the students one more opportunity to completely internalize the skit and cultural differences. A fantasy trip will help them internally visualize what they have learned after they have already edited their unsuccessful attempt at it. This makes the skit and differences part of their world and enables them to use the new behaviors naturally in the future.

Often after a guided imagery, I like to talk to my students about their experience. Here you have the chance to let students compare the guided imagery with the edited movie to see how similar they were. This too provides a good chance for discussion and intensification of the material.

The students can draw a picture of their feelings about this experience while being in their edited movie of their successful use of the new situation. (Many students are able to express their feelings more openly in pictures easier than in words.) In the group, talk about the student's feelings—of course, if a student is not willing to talk about his experience, he should not be forced to.

The generating of new behavior patterns for the learner or even for the native-speaker is extremely important. In a study on communication done at the University of Pennsylvania, it was found that seven percent of what we communicate is the result of the words we use; the content of our communication. Thirty-eight percent of the act of communicating with others is due to verbal behavior, i.e., tone of voice, timbre, tempo, and volume. The rest—fifty-five percent of our communication to others—is a result of non-verbal communication, i.e., body posture, breathing, skin color, and movement (James and Woodsmall). It goes without saying how important new behavior can be for everyone.

Syer and Connolly point out that, "because we have to learn so much of our behavior rather than it's being 'programmed' through instinct or wired into our nervous system, we have a tremendous ability as a species to perform old activities in new ways and even to do new things never before considered possible, perhaps never before imagined" (p. 23).

CHAPTER 6
The Meta-Model

As language teachers, we know that native speakers of a certain language have a special way of perceiving the world. They have a societal "map" of the world, so to speak. Of course, each individual within this group can vary, but he or she stays pretty much within this map or may become an outcast. Realizing that their map of the world is only a *representation* of the world helps us as teachers to better understand our students.

Lewis and Pucelik state that language is the symbolic representation of this map or experience of "our" world. However, this linguistic system is not "only an indicator of how a person creates his model of the world, but it also serves to enhance as well as limit perception" (p. 69).

In NLP, Bandler and Grinder developed the Meta-Model to accommodate this. Leslie Cameron-Bandler describes the Meta-Model as "an explicit set of linguistic information gathering tools designed to reconnect a person's language to the experience that is represented by their language" (p. 223). She goes on to say that ". . . essentially, the Meta-Model serves as an interface between language and experience" (p. 223). This is what language teachers instill in our students when they are learning a new language. The Meta-Model is set up into three categories:

Gathering Information
Who, what, where, when, how specifically?

This is used when information is left out of a learner's dialogue or when it has been unspecified or generalized.

EXAMPLE: Learner might say, "I don't understand." Teacher asks, "What don't you understand?"
EXAMPLE: Learner might say, "It's too difficult for me." Teacher asks, "What's too difficult?"

Can you say that about yourself?
This is used when the learner says something about another person which might apply to himself.
EXAMPLE: Learner says, "He never seems to follow what I'm saying." Teacher says, "Can you say, 'I never seem to follow what he's saying'?" (Taken from Lewis and Pucelik, pp. 110-111.)

By using these concepts, it is possible to clear up any discrepancies between teacher and student so that both parties know what the exact problem or goal might be.

Expanding Limits
What stops you? What would happen if you did?

This is used when you hear words like *can't* or *should.*
EXAMPLE: Learner might say, "I can't do this." Teacher might say, "What stops you from doing it?"

Can you think of a time (situation) when you did (didn't)?
This is used when the learner indicates the belief that there are no exceptions.
EXAMPLE: Learner might say, "I never can do this right." Teacher might ask, "Can you think of a time when you could?" (Taken from Lewis and Pucelik, pp. 111.)

In using these concepts, it is possible to help the learner overcome learning barriers.

Changing Meanings
How do you know?

This is used when the learner is "mind reading."
EXAMPLE: Learner might say, "He should know I can't." Teacher might say, "How should he know?"

How do they (you) make you/them feel that way?
This is used when the learner states cause-effect relationships through another's emotions.
EXAMPLE: Learner might say, "She drives me crazy." Teacher might say, "In what way does she drive you crazy?" (Taken from Lewis and Pucelik, pp. 111-112.)

Following these parameters, it is possible for the teacher to intensify the language experience for the learner by making the language more a real part of the learner's world.

Richardson states that active listening in communication is listening empathically in order to share as much as possible the other person's experience so that you can receive the person's communication in precisely the way it is meant (p. 87).

Actively listening to another person means that you learn to see, hear, and feel much in the same manner as your partner does. However, there are sometimes misunderstandings that can be clarified by simply paraphrasing what your partner has already said. By doing this, the other person often will realize that she or he has left something out.

If this doesn't come to the rescue, the use of the Meta-Model will. In the application of the Meta-Model, Richardson points out that a more effective way to probe for unexpressed or hidden meanings is to ask "what?" questions. He states, "A 'what?' question (and it's variations 'who,' 'which,' 'when,' 'where,' and 'how') asked in a non-threatening tone will usually produce a specific response" (p. 88)—"but 'why' will frequently result in generalizations, rationalizations, denials, or justifications" (p. 89). These results can be, however, very desirable in a language classroom, so we teachers must be very careful with the application of this model.

Using the Meta-Model provides the language teacher with a sound basis for a good discussion. Of course, if you are working with a group, you must be more careful on how far you go with personal questions. Not everyone is pleased to be intensely questioned in front of a group.

An example of using the Meta-Model can be as follows:

When teaching German, I like to first ask students questions about a subject before we read a story about it or do grammar exercises. The subject could deal with a first girlfriend or boyfriend.

Wann haben Sie deine(n) erste(n) Freund(in) gehabt?
   (When did you have your first boy/girlfriend?)
Wo haben Sie ihn/sie kennengelernt?
   (Where did you meet him/her?)
Warum war diese Person so interessant für Sie?
   (Why was this person so interesting for you?)
Welche Eigenschaften dieser Person halten Sie heute noch für wichtig?
   (Which characteristics of this person do you still consider to be important?)

After several questions about the individual's own experience, you can then use Fig. 6.1 (Nervensäge) as an extension of the subject as well as the introduction to the past (use of the participle) in German.

Meta-Model questions can also be used in obtaining information about the characters in the illustration as well as class participants:

Wann haben Sie Ihre Hausaufgaben gemacht?
   (When did you do your homework?)
Wer ist das kleine Mädchen?
   (Who is the little girl?)
Was will die Schwester eigentlich?
   (What does the sister really want?)
Warum schickt der Bruder seine Schwester nicht weg?
   (Why doesn't the brother send away his sister?)
Warum sind der Bruder und seine Freundin so schockiert?
   (Why are the brother and his girlfriend so shocked?)
Was ist eine Nervensäge?
   (What is a Nervensäge?)
Was würden Sie in dieser Situation tun?
   (What would you do in this situation?)

Fig. 6.1 (Nervensäge: taken from Rogers)

Using the Meta-Model with such texts leads to many laughs, a good easy-going atmosphere, and easy learning. Wujec points out that "the best conversations are those in which you focus on the meanings, not the words" (p. 145). Asking such questions as above will divert the learner's attention to meaning and not so much to words or grammar.

My experiences have shown that, on an individual basis, the Meta-Model can be of great value. The learner is so busy with her experiences that she doesn't seem to be really aware of the fact that she is speaking another language. She is more concerned with her problem or situation at hand. In my opinion, this is exactly what language teachers really want. Our students should be as involved as possible in using the language so that it has a natural effect.

By using this model, it is also possible to uncover cultural differences that might otherwise have remained undetected. For example, using the model helped me find out about differences between German and English that were to the advantage of both the learner and myself (a native speaker of English). In English the word "manager" has a rather general application. It can be applied to anyone who manages something. In German, however, the meaning more specifically corresponds to the English word "executive." Through the application of the Meta-Model, differences like this can be quickly and easily overcome, benefitting all parties concerned and leaving the learner with an experience for the language she won't forget for a long time.

In the book *Carnival* by Deborah Spence, the hawker at the carnival perhaps sums up best the effect the Meta-Model can have. "It's about learning more from what people say: it's about asking and learning exactly what someone's saying instead of making up your own versions. It's about asking yourself new questions."

The hawker goes on to say, "Well, when you ask me that, for example, instead of just guessing what I mean, you're getting the feel of this. When you're talking to someone, and they use sentences that leave out something, or make you go inside and guess about what they mean, then the idea is to ask for whatever's left out. That way, you'll learn more about what the other person means, instead of making up your own meanings" (p. 27).

CHAPTER 7
Artwork

Throughout this book I have referred to different drawing exercises to supplement activities such as a fantasy trip, a trance state, etc. The use of artwork in the foreign language classroom is one of your most valuable means of tapping into the students' creative resources and anchoring their experiences and knowledge. Campbell et al. say that "the visual arts clarify and deepen understanding of basic skills" (p. 67).

In her book *Drawing On The Right Side Of The Brain,* Betty Edwards states that drawing provides a twofold advantage. "By gaining access to the part of your mind that works in a style conducive to creative, intuitive thought, you will learn a fundamental skill of visual arts . . . Second, through learning to draw . . . you will gain the ability to think more creatively in other areas of your life" (pp. 14-15).

By drawing in the foreign language classroom, you provide your students the chance to expedite learning a language, and for some, to even be able to express themselves more effectively.

Research has shown that the neocortex of the brain can be divided into right and left hemispheres. For many aspects of language learning, we know that the learner is tapping his left hemisphere; however, for creative activities such as drawing, we know that the learner is using his right hemisphere. By utilizing both hemispheres, you provide your students with a more effective, "whole-brain" opportunity to learn a foreign language.

Charles Faulkner (personal communication) has stated that he finds artwork provides the student with the opportunity to visually and kinesthetically express how he can benefit from attending the course. Using artwork in the foreign language classroom provides the students with the opportunity to use their VAK systems.They can express their expected outcomes visually and kinesthetically—and later auditorially, by explaining their pictures.

Armstrong (1991) states that engaging in different art forms serves to bring out the natural genius in kids. (In adults also—the child within each and every one of us; added by author.) This provides them the chance to express their innermost feelings and thoughts in a visible way. Artwork challenges young and old to design products that respond to the inner stirrings of the soul and the outer demands of the sensory world.

For example, say that you have just completed a fantasy trip "to the beach" to review vocabulary items. Have your students draw a picture for their trip to the beach. This gives them the chance to kinesthetically express themselves through the physical action of drawing a picture and release their emotions/feelings in pictures. I have my students think about how they can express their experience at the beach in English while drawing their picture. The picture fulfills the visual aspect for the artist and later for the other members of the class. Once everyone has completed their pictures, they are given the chance to show their pictures and tell about them or the special experience they represent. The other students are given the chance to ask questions about the picture/experience, thus providing for very interesting conversations. (Don't forget Meta-Model questions!)

In my beginning courses, I like to have my students draw a picture of their imaginary families (see "AS IF "). The teacher can help each student construct his imaginary family by asking questions about their families. First I give my students the chance to tell about their families before asking questions. (See fig. 7.1.) Campbell et al. explain how they use artwork to secure comprehension of material read (paraphrase "Blending the visual and language arts" p. 68) by making puppets or drawing the main characters to symbolize personality traits and/or physical characteristics.

Fig. 7: Lisa's Family

More advanced students are often able and interested in learning how to express their feelings. So I give them the chance by playing them a piece of classical music while they relax in their chairs. When the piece is over, I have them draw a picture (abstract, true-to-life, whatever) which illustrates the feelings they had while listening. While they are drawing, I play the piece again. Then we look at the pictures and talk about them and what they express.

For beginners, a similar exercise is appropriate. I like to use *The Four Seasons* by Vivaldi. Have your students fold a piece of blank paper so that they have four squares/parts. In each part, they draw a picture for each season while listening to the music. Each season is labelled accordingly, and I then ask each student questions about their pictures such as "What's your favorite thing to do in spring?" or "What is your favorite food in winter?" (Meta-Model questions). It is possible to involve all VAK aspects. To intensify the learner's experience, have them pantomime their favorite season or their favorite activity for their favorite season, and the others guess which season and what activity it is.

Another way to teach vocabulary to express emotions is to make masks. I first have each student pick two emotions (from a list already provided and discussed). Often I suggest they pick one positive and one negative emotion that is typical for them personally. Each student makes a mask to represent each emotion. Once they are finished, we talk about each mask and what it represents and means. To end this exercise, I have each student pick one of his two emotions. The students form groups of two and invent a dialogue between their masks (emotions). What do these masks say to each other? How do they react? This turns into a play between the two masks.

To learn the different parts of the body, you can play "Simon Says." Once you have introduced the parts of the body, give your students a blank piece of paper and have them fold a third of it back. On this third, have them draw a head in any way they want—a small part of the neck must show on the rest of the paper so the next artist knows where the neck ends. Now each student gives his drawing to his neighbor (paper folded so that the neighbor cannot see the head). This student again folds the paper in third and draws a torso in any way he wants on the middle third. This student indicates where the torso stops on the bottom third so the next student can draw the legs and feet. Once this "being" is complete, collect all the pictures, show them to the whole class, and return the picture to the person who drew the head. The students can label the different parts of the body on their "being." (See Figure 7.2.)

Another possibility to learn parts of the body is to give a group of two students two pieces of butcher paper. Each piece is longer than the tallest person in the group. One student lies down on one piece of butcher paper, and the other student traces around his partner. The same is done for the other person in the group. After completing this, the "bodies" are hung up and each student labels the different parts of his/her own body.

For advanced students, you can do an exercise at the end of the course which deals with personality traits. The students have to work in pairs. Each student must think of a positive trait in his personality and draw a picture for it (realistic, abstract or whatever). Once this is done, the other student in the pair draws a picture for a positive trait in his partner's personality. After completing this, show the picture the student drew for his positive point as well as the picture his partner drew for the first

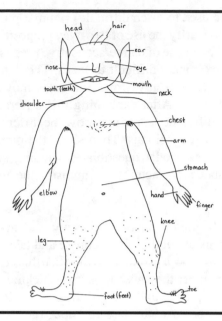

Figure 7.2: "Being" (parts of the body)

student's positive point. With your students, compare the points and talk about the similarities in the two pictures.

You can also work with mobiles to reinforce vocabulary. In a German course I taught, I had my students decide if they wanted to work with animals, fruits, vegetables, or modes of transportation. They chose animals, and I had them draw five or six different pictures of animals we had learned. Then we talked about the pictures (of course in rather simple terms) and then I had them construct a mobile with their pictures.

Another art game to learn vocabulary is to make pictures of words. To do this, write different words on pieces of paper and put them in a bag. For beginners, these can be simple words like *chair, pen, tree,* etc. For advanced learners, more complicated words like *freedom, happiness, proceed,* etc. can be used, and for English For Special Purposes, words like *lathe, bevel, drilling machine,* etc. One member of the class takes a word from the bag and does not show it to anyone. She then draws a picture of the word while the other students try to guess what it is. This can be done individually or in teams.

Art can even be used to teach difficult grammar points. Hager (1991) uses drawings to clarify the use of two-way prepositions in German. In German the different use of dative/accusative prepositions like "in, an, zwischen" are extremely difficult to learn. The dative form indicates location while the accusative form indicates movement. Figure 7.3 shows this difference. After explaining this difference, have the students draw two different pictures to show the difference in meaning of selected two-way prepositions. Then show the pictures to the whole class and use Meta-Model questions (including submodalities; see Hager 1991) about the pictures to intensify the understanding (see ANCHORING).

At the end of a beginning course, I give my students a blank postcard. I tell them to think about the whole course and take one positive thing or experience and draw a picture to symbolize this. They can draw their picture in any manner they wish (abstract, stickmen, etc.). Then each one explains their picture to the rest of the class. After this, I collect the cards and give one to each class member (never the picture to its creator). Then I have the person with the card write his real name and address on the card in the right position for the addressee. After that, I collect the cards again and give the card back to its original artist. Then the artist writes a postcard to the addressee on the card and tells about his experience at the English course. Once everyone has completed his letter, I collect the cards, and several days after the course is finished, I send the cards to the persons the cards are addressed to. This functions both as a good memory and a souvenir from the course.

Crowley and Mills point out "in our real world, we perceive a horse as a horse. Yet, in the world of fantasy and mythology, with added wings, the horse becomes Pegasus, who can transport the beholder to all parts of the world in unlimited ways. How limited we really are by everyday reality. How incredibly free we become when entering the world of fantasy" (p. 14).

Der Mann geht <u>ins</u> Kino. **Der Mann sitzt <u>im</u> Kino.**

Figure 7.3: Dative/Accusative Prepositions
(Taken from Hager, 1991)

Bibliography

Anderson, Jill. *Thinking, Changing, Rearranging*. Portland Oregon: Metamorphous Press, 1988.

Andreas, Steve and Connirae Andreas. *Change Your Mind And Keep The Change*. Moab, UT: Real People Press, 1987.

Andreas, Steve and Connirae Andreas. *Heart of the Mind*. Moab, UT: Real People Press, 1989.

Armstrong, Thomas. *In Their Own Way*. Los Angeles: Jeremy P. Tarcher, Inc., 1987.

_____, *Awakening Your Child's Natural Genius*. New York: G. P. Putnam's Sons, 1991.

Bandler, Richard and John Grinder. *Frogs Into Princes*. Moab, UT: Real People Press, 1979.

Bandler, Richard and Will MacDonald. *An Insider's Guide to Sub-Modalities*. Cupertino, CA: Meta Publications, 1988.

Barker, Joel Arthur. *Paradigms: The Business of Discovering the Future*. New York: HarperBusiness, 1993.

Belknap, Martha. *Taming Your Dragons*. New York: D.O.K. Publishers, 1986.

Bry, Adelaide. *Visualization: Directing the Movies of Your Mind*. New York: Harper and Row Publishers, 1972.

Cameron-Bandler, Leslie. *Solutions*. San Rafael, CA: Future Pace, Inc., 1985.

Campbell, Linda, Bruce Campbell, and Dee Dickinson. *Teaching and Learning Through Multiple Intelligences*. Seattle, WA: New Horizons for Learning, 1992.

Cleveland, Bernard. *Master Teaching Techniques*. Muskego, WI: The Connecting Link Press, 1986.

Crowley, Richard and Joyce Mills. *Cartoon Magic*. New York: Maginations Press, 1989.

Davis, Martha et al. *The Relaxation and Stress Reduction Workbook*. Oakland, CA: New Harbinger Publications, 1988.

DeMille, Richard. *Put Your Mother on the Ceiling*. Middlesex: Penguin Books Ltd., 1986.

Dhority, Lynn. *Moderne Suggestopaedie*. Bremen/Germany: PLS-Verlag, 1986.

Dilts, Robert. "EEG and Representational Systems" in *Roots of Neuro-Linguistic Programming*. Cupertino, CA: Meta Publications, 1983, pp. 3-57.

Dilts, Robert, and Jeremy David Green. "Applications of Neuro-Linguistic Programming in Family Therapy and Interpersonal Negotiation" in*Applications of Neuro-Linguistic Programming,* ed. Robert Dilts. Cupertino, CA: Meta Publications, 1983, pp. 1-71.

Edwards, Betty. *Drawing on the Right Side of the Brain*. Los Angeles: J.P. Tarcher Inc., 1979.

Galgean, Beverly-Collene. *Mind Sight Learning Through Imaging*. Santa Barbara, CA: Center for Integrative Learning, 1983.

Goodrich, Janet. *Natural Vision Improvement*. Berkeley, CA: Celestial Arts, 1986.

Grinder, Michael. *Righting the Educational Conveyor Belt*. Portland, Oregon: Metamorphous Press, 1989.

Hager, Michael. "Learning Verb Tenses with NLP," in*Praxis des neusprachlichen Unterrichts*, IV, 1989.

_____, "Learning Vocabulary with the Help of NLP," in *Praxis des neusprachlichen Unterrichts*, I, 1990a.

_____, "The Use of Timeline in Teaching," *Journal of the Society for Accelerated Learning and Teaching*, 15 (3&4), 1990b, pp. 133-137.

_____, "The Use of Drawing in the Language Classroom," *Fremdsprachen lehren and lernen*, 20, 1991, pp. 231-233.

_____, "Superlearning in Adult Education," *Fremd/Sprachen/ Unterricht*, 1, 1993a, pp. 29-30.

_____, "Different Kinds of Learners and Techniques for Learning Vocabulary," *Fremd/Sprachen/Unterricht* , 7, 1993b, pp. 392-392.

Hutchison, Michael. *Mega Brain*. New York: Ballantine, 1986.

Jackson, June. *Following Instructions*. Denver, CO: New Learning Pathways, 1983.

Jacobson, Sid. *Meta-Cation I*. Cupertino, CA: Meta Publications, 1983.

James, Tad and Wyatt Woodsmall. *Time Line Therapy*. Cupertino, CA: Meta Publications, 1988.

Jensen, Eric.*Super-Teaching*. Del Mar, CA: Turning Point For Teachers, 1988.

Laborde, Genie.*Influencing with Integrity*. Palo Alto, CA; Syntony Publishing, 1987.

Laborde, Genie. *Fine Tune Your Brain*. Palo Alto, CA: Syntony Publishing, 1988.

Lankton, Steve. *Practical Magic*. Cupertino, CA: Meta Publications, 1980.

Lewis, Byron and Frank Pucelik.*Magic of NLP Demystified*. Portland, Oregon: Metamorphous Press, 1982.

Lloyd, Linda.*Classroom Magic*. Portland, Oregon: Metamorphous Press 1984.

Lofland, Donald J. *Powerlearning*. Stanford, CT: Longweadow Press, 1992.

Markova, Dawna.*How Your Child Is Smart*. Berkeley, CA: Conari Press, 1992.

Moore, Robin. *Awakening The Hidden Storyteller*. Boston: Shambhala Publications. Inc. 1991.

Murphy, Joseph. *The Power of Your Subconscious Mind*. Englewood Cliffs, NJ: Prentice-Hall, 1963.

O'Connor, Joseph. *Not Pulling Strings*. Portland, Oregon: Metamorphous Press, 1989.

Richardson, Jerry. *The Magic of Rapport*. Cupertino, CA: Meta Publications, 1987.

Ristad, Eloise. *A Soprano on Her Head*. Moab, UT: Real People Press, 1982.
Rogers, Paul and Jeremy Long. *Alles klar*. Walton-on-Thames, Surrey: Thomas Nelson and Sons, Ltd., 1985.

Rose, Colin. *Accelerated Learning*. England: Topaz Publishing Limited, 1985.

Schmid, Charles. *New Dimensions in Learning*. San Francisco: LIND-Institute, 1985.

Sinetar, Marsha. *Developing A 21st-Century Mind*. New York: Ballantine Books, 1991.

Spence, Deborah. *The Carnival*. Indian Rocks Beach, FL: Southern Institute Press, Inc. 1987.

Spolin, Viola. *Theater Games for the Classroom: A Teacher's Handbook*. Evanston, IL: Northwestern University Press, 1986.

Syer, John and Christopher Connolly. *Sporting Body Sporting Mind*. Englewood Cliffs, NJ: Prentice Hall, 1987.

Van Nagel, C. et al., *Mega-Teaching and Learning*. Portland, Oregon: Metamorphous Press, 1993.

Whitmore, Diana. *Psychosynthesis in Education*. Wellingborough, Northamptonshire: Turnstone Press Ltd., 1986.

Williams, Linda. *Teaching for the Two-Sided Mind*. New York: Simon and Schuster Inc., 1983.

Wujec, Tom. *Pumping Ions*. Toronto: Doubleday, 1988.

Recommended Reading

Chapter 1

Magic of NLP Demystified by Lewis and Pucelik provides a good overview and introduction to Neurolinguistic Programming for those who have little or no knowledge about the technology. This book is more for therapists but the premises about representational systems and building rapport through the use of VAK are good.

Influencing With Integrity by Genie Laborde is a good source for using NLP for business. But many aspects of this book can be used as good background for teachers. Laborde's exercises and explanations are of good quality.

Not Pulling Strings by Joseph O'Connor is also a good overview and introduction to NLP, applied to teaching music. The examples and exercises are applicable to teaching other subject areas.

How Your Child Is Smart by Dawna Markova is interesting for how Markova classifies learners according to their preferences for the different representational systems. Her ideas about the application of conscious and subconscious use of the representational systems is a little difficult to accept. But in general this book can be beneficial to those who are interested in learner classifications.

In Their Own Way by Thomas Armstrong is a very good resource book for classroom exercises using our different senses. These exercises for teaching all subject areas are applicable for adults as well as children. As well, this book is a very good introduction to Howard Gardner's theory of multiple intelligences and how to classify learners according to it.

Chapter 2

Influencing With Integrity is a source for additional information on the use of "As If."

Chapter 3

Visualization by Adelaide Bry is a very good introduction to fantasy trips. She goes into great detail about how to use fantasy trips in different ways for different purposes.

Mind Sight by Beverly-Colleene Galyean is a good source of different kinds of fantasy trips for teaching children different subject areas. Her book is also a good introduction to the teaching method "Confident Teaching."

Sporting Body Sporting Mind by Syer and Connolly is an excellent book for understanding the most important aspects of visualization but in reference to sports; aspects of teaching sports are included.

The books *Taming Your Dragons* by Martha Belknap and *Put Your Mother On The Ceiling* by Richard De Mille are good sources for ready-made fantasy trips of various kinds. Belknap's "trips" are more for relaxation than directly teaching school subject matter.

Chapter 4

Time Line Therapy by James and Woodsmall is an introduction to using timelines in therapy. It provides a good background to the theory and use of timelines but not in teaching.

Chapter 5

Sporting Body Sporting Mind by Syer and Connolly provides good examples of how to use the New Behavior Generator in sports.

Paradigms by Joel Arthur Barker is a good source about paradigms in the business world. Understanding the background and use of paradigms provides a great deal of insight for the use of the New Behavior Generator and how behavior can be changed.

Chapter 6
Magic of NLP Demystified by Lewis and Pucelik has a good chapter about the Meta-Model and how this theory can be used in therapy.

Chapter 7
Drawing On The Right Side of The Brain by Betty Edwards is a good source for background information on techniques for teaching drawing. The chapters on the use of our two hemispheres in the neocortex to teach drawing are very interesting for the person who is not so familiar with the theory of the right and left hemispheres.

Glossary

Accessing cues—movements of the eyes which represent the mental processes of retrieving thoughts and experiences stored in the brain.

Anchor—a certain stimulus which produces a certain response when it is applied.

"As if . . ."—strategy used to pretend or act as if one is someone else or doing something one is normally unable to do.

Associated—when one is in his/herself (body) while having experiences.

Auditory—dealing with hearing or speaking. This can be either internal or external.

Body Language—the way we communicate with others through the movements and postures of our body.

Constraints—filters used on the model-building processes. There are three different kinds; neurological, social, and individual.

Disassociated or **Dissociated**—when one is outside of him/herself (body) while having experiences. In this position, one is able to see or watch him/herself.

External—dealing with anything going on outside of oneself.

4-Tuple—a moment in time encompassing all the representational systems; visual, auditory, kinesthetic, olfactory, and gustatory.

Individual Constraints—the collection of our personal past, this is a complete set of stored and remembered experiences. The complete set works as a filter for any new or ongoing experiences.

Internal—dealing with anything going on inside oneself.

Kinesthetic—dealing with the body or emotions/feelings. This can be either internal or external.

Lead System—the representational system which leads one into his/her preferred system for storing information.

Meta-Model—a linguistic tool which can be used to obtain a more complete representation of the person's intended response, idea, or feeling about someone or something.

Modeling—the representing of a thing or process to better aid in understanding what it represents. It can also aid in predicting how this will operate in different situations.

Monitor Model—Stephen Krashen's theory about how language learners develop an internal mechanism for monitoring and correcting their production (semantic, syntactic and phonological) of a foreign/second language.

Neurological Constraint—our mental and sensory filters.

New Behavior Generator—a strategy to develop awareness of other ways of doing some given task and how to habitualize the use of this new information.

Preferred Representational System—the system which one prefers to use the most to process and access information or experiences.

Representational Systems—representations of experience through our different senses: visual, auditory, kinesthetic, olfactory and gustatory.

State—any of a number of mental processes happening within a person at one given time.

Resource State—being in an experience in which one is extremely resourceful and/or confident.

Stuck State—being in an experience loop and not being able to get out of this loop.

Trance State—being so intensely involved in an experience that one is not aware of anything going on outside of this experience. Similar to dozing or daydreaming.

Strategy—a sequence of mental processes to reach a goal/target/aim.

Sub-modality—detailed characteristics of the representational systems. For example, visual—hue or brightness; auditory—loudness or timbre; kinesthetic—temperature or texture.

Timeline—a mental organization of memories in relation to time.

Trigger—a stimulus which activates an anchor.

Visual—dealing with the eyes and seeing. This can be either internal or external.

Index

Metamorphous Press

Metamorphous Press is a publisher of books and other media providing resources for personal growth and positive change. MP publishes leading-edge ideas that help people strengthen their unique talents and discover that we are responsible for our own realities.

Many of our titles center around Neurolinguistic Programming (NLP). NLP is an exciting, practical, and powerful communication model that has been able to connect observable patterns of behavior and communication and the processes that underlie them.

Metamorphous Press provides selections in many useful subject areas such as communication, health and fitness, education, business and sales, therapy, selections for young persons, and other subjects of general and specific interest. Our products are available in fine bookstores around the world.

Our distributors for North America are:

Baker & Taylor	M.A.P.S.	Pacific Pipeline
Bookpeople	Moving Books	the distributors
Ingram	New Leaf	Sage Book Distributors

For those of you overseas, we are distributed by:

Airlift (UK, Western Europe)
Specialist Publications (Australia)

New selections are added regularly and availability and prices change, so call for a current catalog or to be put on our mailing list. If you have difficulty finding our products in your favorite bookstore, or if you prefer to order by mail, we will be happy to make our books and other products available to you directly. Please call or write us at:

Metamorphous Press
P.O. Box 10616   Portland, OR 97210-0616
TEL (503) 228-4972
FAX (503) 223-9117

TOLL FREE ORDERING
1-800-937-7771

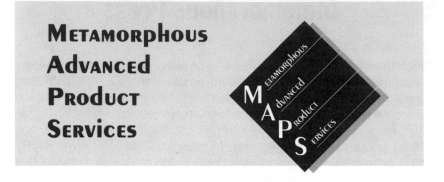

METAMORPHOUS ADVANCED PRODUCT SERVICES (M.A.P.S.) is the master distributor for Metamorphous Press and other fine publishers.

M.A.P.S. offers books, cassettes, videos, software, and miscellaneous products in the following subjects; Bodywork, Business & Sales; Children; Education; Enneagram; Health; (including Alexander Technique and Rolfing); Hypnosis; Personal Development; Psychology (including Neurolinguistic Programming); and Relationships/Sexuality.

If you cannot find our books at your favorite bookstore, you can order directly from M.A.P.S.

TO ORDER OR REQUEST A FREE CATALOG

MAIL   M.A.P.S.
        P.O. Box 10616
        Portland, OR 97210-0616

FAX   (503) 223-9117

CALL   Toll free 1-800-233-MAPS

CUSTOMER SERVICE AND ALL OTHER BUSINESS

CALL   (503) 228-4972